What others are saying about
Doyle Dykes and *The Lights of Marfa*

When I think of Doyle, "generosity" immediately comes to mind. He once sent me a card containing three Bible verses, each dealing with giving. His book, as well as his exceptional ability on the guitar, is an expression of how he walks the talk and gives to others without holding anything back. After listening to Doyle play the guitar, you know his talent comes from a stronger, higher power. We are all blessed because of his willingness to share his life and talent with us. When I grow up I want to be just like Doyle (and play like him too).
Roy Clark – Grammy award–winning member of the Grand Ole Opry and Country Music Hall of Fame

This book by my favorite guitarist is as captivating as Doyle's music.
Rick Warren – Senior Pastor, Saddleback Church

Doyle is a great man of God who writes in a personal way, shares so many of the experiences and stories that have shaped his life, warms our hearts with his gentle ways, uplifts us with his strong faith, leads us with a thundering velvet touch, and…oh, yeah, he also plays guitar very well! We love you, Doyle.
Tommy Emmanuel – Guitarist, composer, CGP, and certified Doyle fan!

Doyle Dykes is not only one of my favorite guitar players—he's one of my favorite people. Anything he does is gonna be great. He's had an amazing life!
Ricky Skaggs – Grammy award–winning recording artist

Doyle Dykes has reached the outer limits of guitar theory and performance. In *The Lights of Marfa* he reveals an even higher attainment. Through his inspiring life experiences he has learned the true meaning of things that really matter – things like family, prayer, the Bible, and se̶ ̶ ̶King of kings. This is a book worth reading. I know because I've re
R. Lamar Vest – President/CEO, American

One of the highlights in my life as a guita̶ ̶ ̶ to Doyle play his guitar unto the Lord. H̶ ̶ ̶ me. With all that talent, there is deep within Do̶y̶l̶ ̶ ̶ and Savior, and when I'm with him, I know I'm in the p̶r̶ ̶ ̶ who loves his God, wife and children, and his country. He also truly me̶n̶t̶o̶rs thousands of musicians musically and spiritually, encouraging them to play well, love well, and serve well. It's been an honor for me to record with him, too. I rejoice in getting to know a brother who has a wonderful story about God's amazing grace in his life and music. Thank you, Doyle, for writing this book.
Phil Keaggy – Award-winning contemporary Christian guitarist, songwriter, and producer

"Master of His Craft" – "Christian Gentleman" – "Loyal Friend." These are just a few of the qualities I see in Doyle Dykes, a man I consider it an honor to call "Friend." You will be enlightened and encouraged by the accounts contained in the volume you now hold in your hand. Enjoy it!

Dr. Donnie Sumner – *Gospel artist, vocal arranger for Elvis Presley,*
and owner of Sumner Associates

Doyle is the type of person you meet for five minutes and you feel you have been friends for a lifetime. You'll find his stories equally as captivating and heartwarming.

Eric Johnson – *Platinum-selling, Grammy award–winning artist*

Doyle Dykes has the rare gift of being able to touch our hearts with his music. When he plays the guitar, the angels sing along! His new book, *The Lights of Marfa*, touches us in a different way. It brings us closer to God – by way of Doyle's unique perspective and vision. It's a blessing!

Michael Lloyd – *Multiple award–winning Hollywood record producer and composer*

Doyle Dykes is an original and so is this delightful book. It tells the story of a talented, unpretentious man in an interesting and honest way. For the many people who, like me, have always admired Doyle's artistry with a guitar, this book will be a fascinating look inside his life. I enjoyed it immensely.

Dr. Paul Conn – *President, Lee University*

Doyle has told me that via "Classical Gas," I was one of his early inspirations. He later become a inspiration for me! We played together at Dan Crary's "Primal Twang" in September 2006. Doyle's performances were highlights of the evening. All the other musicians and the crew stopped what we were doing to watch and hear him play. He continues to explore the frontiers of music for the guitar and the frontiers of spiritual expression as well. He is a major inspiration for pickers of all persuasions, young and old alike!

Mason Williams – *Recording artist*

Doyle has been a great blessing to our church in Seattle. Doyle walks with God because he always has a great spirit and a song from the Lord, and brings excellence to every service. His music is a gift that blesses so many – and his friendship is an even greater gift. He is an anointed, godly minstrel. This book will lift, encourage, and bless you to live a godly life on a higher level.

Casey Treat – *Founding pastor of Christian Faith Center, Seattle, Washington*

Doyle Dykes and I met each other in the mid-'70s and I tell people that he was better then than I'll be in my next life. This book is not only about a phenomenal guitarist but a man with unquestioning love for his family and God. *The Lights of Marfa* shines with spiritual inspiration as he shares his life's adventures and miracles of faith. A must-read for everyone wishing to benefit from his unfaltering devotion.

Jeff Carlisi – *Founding member of 38 Special, cofounder of Camp Jam*

I have been fortunate enough to play with many great guitarists over the years, but there simply is no one else who does what Doyle does on the instrument. But that's not all. His unashamed spirituality is as real as it gets, and I love the way he seamlessly integrates it into his music and live performances. It is such a pleasure to stand beside him onstage and tap into that deep well of music and love he so effortlessly shares with those around him, allowing us to hang on for the ride! His book, *The Lights of Marfa*, is no exception. It captures his vision of life, love, music, and spirituality in a way as unique as he is.

Dave Pomeroy – *Bassist/producer, president of the Nashville Musicians Association, AFM Local 257*

I could not put this book down. While reading, I recalled some of those wonderful nights at the Opry when the Lord's presence filled the Opry house – like when Haley sang "Amazing Grace" or Doyle seemed to become one with his guitar and spirit. He always blessed my heart along with so many of the artists and musicians. His gift is so great and his humbleness and faithfulness take it to unbelievable heights. Thank you for writing this fabulous book and sharing Jesus through your life experiences.

Bob Whittaker – *Former general manager of the Grand Ole Opry*

For several years, Doyle has been nice enough to stay up late and share his rare talent through music and stories with us and our listeners. We've also been privileged to join him onstage at several concerts, and in special off-stage moments, and have come to understand this gentle man is the real deal. The treasure of his friendship is something we don't take lightly. With the wonderful stories Doyle shares in *The Lights of Marfa* you'll come to know, as we have, he doesn't just "talk the talk" but, in fact, "walks the walk." And you'll be very glad you made the journey with him.

Steve King & Johnnie Putman – *WGN Radio, Chicago*

Doyle is this generation's Chet Atkins – and I was a friend of Chet's so I can say that! And he's taken it to another level in this book by "shedding light" on his life journey. He intertwines faith, family, Texas, Elvis, Rick Warren, pickers, grinners, believers, sinners, influences, incidents, Bob Taylor tales, straps, tubes, strings, amps, guitars, Bibles, and mysterious Marfian lights, almost like the handful of strings he plucks at the speed of sound in one of his mind-blowing arpeggios! The impossible all comes together in a sweep of inspired grace, both onstage with Doyle and his guitar and in the riffs of his life played out in these pages – all with true humility, heart and soul.

David Pack – *Grammy award–winning recording artist, producer, and FOC CGP (Friend of Chet's, Certified Guitar Player)*

I have known Doyle for a long time. He is not only one of the greatest guitarists of our day, he is a also great person. In *The Lights of Marfa*, he lets us see the man behind the musician and his personal experiences shaped by the greatness and grace of God. Everyone will enjoy reading his rich stories of faith.

Dr. David Cooper – *Senior Pastor, Mount Paran Church, Atlanta, Georgia*

Doyle Dykes is one of the great guitar players of our time. His melodic approach and great technique are only mirrored by his heart for people. He spreads a great light on us, and through his stories and adventures in this book, he leads us to the Source.

Larry Thomas – CEO, Fender Musical Instrument Corporation

Doyle ministers with a humble pastor's heart and a highly skilled musician's hands. He's played at several of our Christian Musician Summit Conferences over the years and I'm constantly amazed as I watch the audience's jaws just drop as they realize the talent they're witnessing. Doyle is a remarkable performer and an effective minister, simply by being himself!

Bruce Adolph – Producer, Christian Music Summit Conferences; publisher, Christian Musician *magazine*

From the mysteries of God to the Lights of Marfa, no one tells a great story quite like Doyle. This book is filled with true stories you will want to read again and tell others – stories that light your soul, light your path, and warm your heart.

Dan Reiland – Executive Pastor, 12 Stone Church, Lawrenceville, Georgia

Doyle has played at Saddleback more than any other guest artist in history. He is an amazing guitarist and has impacted thousands of musicians and non-musicians with his music. He is also a man of deep faith and a master storyteller. *The Lights of Marfa* is a compelling book that will capture your imagination and inspire your faith and love for God.

Rick Muchow – Pastor of Worship, Saddleback Church

Our pilgrimage on this earth is filled with divine appointments all too often unperceived because of the static and pace of life makes us miss the vertical. Wonderfully, Doyle portrays how a loving heavenly Father stoops down and brings LIGHT to our daily experiences. Thank you, Doyle, for this delightful collection of encounters lit by His presence. I will read it again and again.

Joe Focht – Pastor, Calvary Chapel of Philadelphia

There is so much love in this book, so many wonderful tales and so much inspiration, not only for musicians, but also for fathers, sons, and husbands everywhere. Doyle finger-picks stories from his life with as much alacrity as from the strings of his guitar – a treat for all with an appreciation of music and life. Just as his music lifts hearts worldwide – so too now his words, with a wealth of inspirational stories from his extraordinary life. And as I say when I watch him play – I can't fathom how he just did that!

Lord Henry Lytton Cobbold – Screenwriter, producer, and occupant of Knebworth House, Hertfordshire, England

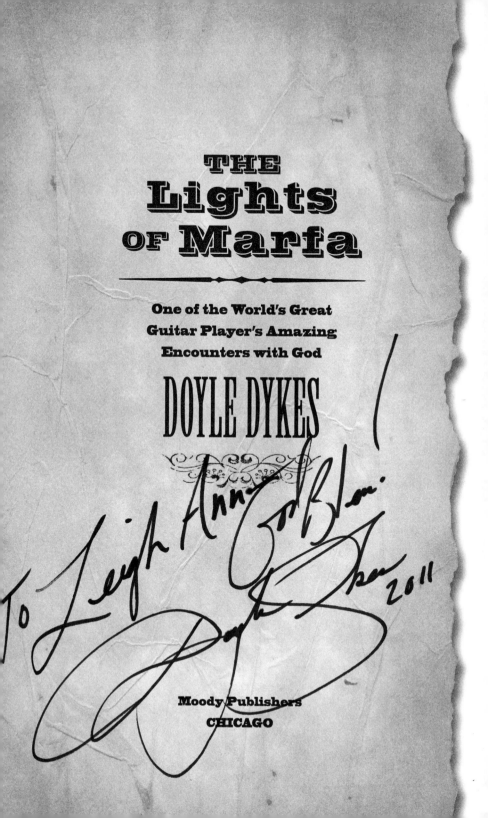

THE Lights OF Marfa

One of the World's Great
Guitar Player's Amazing
Encounters with God

DOYLE DYKES

Moody Publishers
CHICAGO

Unless otherwise indicated, Scripture quotations are taken from the *New King James Version*. Copyright © 1982 by Thomas Nelson, Inc. Used by permission. All rights reserved.

Scripture quotations marked NLT are taken from the *Holy Bible, New Living Translation,* copyright © 1996, 2004. Used by permission of Tyndale House Publishers, Inc., Wheaton, Illinois 60189, U.S.A. All rights reserved.

Scripture quotations marked AMP are taken from *The Amplified Bible*. Copyright © 1965, 1987 by The Zondervan Corporation. *The Amplified New Testament* copyright © 1958, 1987 by The Lockman Foundation. Used by permission.

Scripture quotations marked KJV are taken from the King James Version.

Library of Congress Cataloging-in-Publication Data

Dykes, Doyle.
  The lights of Marfa : one of the world's great guitar player's amazing encounters with God / Doyle Dykes.
    p. cm.
  ISBN 978-0-8024-0037-6
  1. Dykes, Doyle. 2. Guitarists--United States--Biography. 3. Music--Religious aspects. I. Marfa (Tex.) II. Title.
  ML419.D95L54 2011
  787.87092--dc22
    [B]
                          2011001270

Edited by Betsey Newenhuyse
Cover design: Barb Fisher, LeVan Fisher Design
Interior design: Julia Ryan/www.DesignByJulia.com
Photo credits: Holli Brown at Madame Brown Photography
DVD: Bryan Fowler at Fowler Films
Photo on page 214 © by Bryan Fowler
Cover photos © hansjn, Santiago Cornej, and ixe/Shutterstock Images

We hope you enjoy this book from Moody Publishers. Our goal is to provide high-quality, thought-provoking books and products that connect truth to your real needs and challenges. For more information on other books and products written and produced from a biblical perspective, go to www.moodypublishers.com or write to:

Moody Publishers
820 N. LaSalle Boulevard
Chicago, IL 60610

1 3 5 7 9 10 8 6 4 2

Printed in the United States of America

In Dedication

This book is dedicated to my wife, Rita. No one understands me better
than she does. She is uniquely perfect in every way to be my soul mate.
I only hope I can be as good of a husband, best friend, and blessing to her that
she is and has been to me. Although I know that's impossible, I still enjoy trying.
She was the most beautiful and popular girl in school and yet she married me!
I still don't quite understand that but I'm glad she did! She and our children have
truly been my living "Marfa Lights" all these years. She has been a remarkable,
inexplicable, and extraordinary blessing in my life. We are living out our dream,
and that simply means to always be together. She is . . . in a word . . ."Lovely."
Although her heavenly Father is the only father she's ever known,
I believe He especially agrees that I dedicate this book to her.

8TH GRADE TALENT SHOW, KIRBY JUNIOR HIGH, 1968.
RITA WAS THE MOST POPULAR GIRL AT SCHOOL AND
I THOUGHT I HAD NO CHANCE WITH SOMEONE AS
BEAUTIFUL AS SHE WAS. THE LORD HAD OTHER PLANS!

Contents

A Special Word from Bob Taylor

When the big earthquake hits I want to be close to Doyle Dykes. I'm not saying I want him to be in the middle of the BIG ONE, but I think I might have a better chance of surviving in his vicinity. That's because it seems that God is looking after Doyle.

On the other hand, we at Taylor Guitars like to call him "Doppler Doyle" because everywhere he goes he seems to have a knack for driving into some the biggest storms of the year. I'll bet he might have enough rain miles to trade in his driver's license for a boat operator's license.

Doyle and I have talked, emailed, or texted each other a few times a week for well over ten years. We've gotten to know each other pretty well. I've seen him in concert a couple hundred times. I've traveled with him in foreign countries. I've helped him stick his leg with Imitrex pens to relieve the delirious pain from headaches that stopped all functions of his body except the ability to throw up, as he recovered from brain surgery that took the hearing from his right ear. Then, a few hours later, he's onstage doing a fabulous job, and later I tease him about what it took to get him there. He could only remember the half of it.

I saw him heal from that.

I've seen Doyle wow an audience of five hundred Japanese guitar enthusiasts (with a typhoon raging outside, of course), and afterward, I've heard members of the audience try to explain to me what they experienced when Doyle played. They understand the word "ministry" when I offer it up, and nod in agreement with a hearty "Yes!"

I've played banjo at Saddleback Church with Doyle; me enjoying all of the fun and none of the responsibility of playing in front of thousands of people, still sounding good, even with my fading banjo chops due to years of little practice, because Doyle knows how to lay down cover with his guitar that makes a musical space where an amateur like me can look like he knows what he's doing. I like looking like I know what I'm doing.

I like the way Doyle loves guitars. He's into the little subtle details, like the exact color for a stain or where the strap pin is located. His guitars always look immaculate and are always in tip-top condition for a performance. His guitar straps are works of art and he likes his cowboy boots to match. You know those movies where the special forces spy gets ready for his work; where the guy is organized and has the perfect tool in the perfect place, and he wears the right clothes, and has it all together, leaving nothing to chance? That's what Doyle's guitars remind me of.

Then, after a performance, he emails me a video of him and his grandkids; total goofball videos, of him in his other happy-place.

Doyle has a special talent, because he's a guitar player's guitar player. Even the most famous, talented, celebrity guitar players think of him as a master. And yet, he appeals to the person who might be hearing guitar for the very first time. You don't have to be a connoisseur of guitar music to enjoy his songs. They are complicated, and executed with incredible skill, and yet you can hum along. It's amazing. Very few players have that ability. Doyle never plays music that is over the heads of his audience.

One thread that is woven throughout my experience with Doyle is how he can see God's involvement in his life. Many of us miss the intervention that God works on our behalf. Doyle doesn't. He's very aware of that and shares those stories.

The Lights of Marfa is a book full of these stories. When some people write a book it takes all of their life's experience to fill the pages. Not so with Doyle, because there's lots more tales of amazing things that

BOB TAYLOR AND ME AT HIS BEACH HOUSE OUTSIDE OF SAN DIEGO, CA. (2006)

have happened to him. He's only sharing some of them.

He wrote how Eric Johnson, another master musician, recovered his famously stolen guitars, missing for twenty-some years, and how he came upon them while doing a favor for Doyle. It's good to be around Doyle. Maybe God just trusts Doyle to tell the story right so He gives him lots of stories to share.

I love Doyle Dykes. He's my brother and friend. He teaches me things that allow my own deficiencies to be bolstered. He tells me tales that honor God and inspire me to see things through different eyes and tell some stories of my own.

And then he plays his guitar and I'm speechless for a while.

—**Bob Taylor**
Cofounder, Taylor Guitars

INTRODUCTION

How This Book Was Born

A few years ago Steve Lyon from Moody Publishers approached me after a performance in Chicago about writing a book. I'll never forget standing there on the sidewalk and thinking, *Wow, is he speaking to me?* I kept this idea pretty much to myself for several years—until now.

Bob Taylor of Taylor Guitars[1] has been a close friend of mine for over fifteen years now. At one time he served on his pastor John Maxwell's board and was on the worship team at his church for over twenty years. When we get together, we of course talk about guitars, because we both have a passion for that instrument, and thank God that we have certain gifts and talents and the desire to use them in the right way. However, even more often we talk about God, our families, our dogs, banjos, Airstream trailers, camping (he's the desert rat and camping king), friends, and travels we share.

Recently I was at Bob's personal workshop in El Cajon, California, watching him finish a beautiful solid walnut table he was building for his new home. His skills and talents are so diverse—as well as his knowledge of interesting things in general—he'll keep you entertained for hours. Because he is also a spiritual person, I asked Bob if he'd help me pray about this very book you're reading, since I had been struggling to put all these things in my head together in a way that could make sense to people.

Let me say right here that some things will never make sense to us, even the very attributes of God like His peace that "passes all understanding" and His ways not being our ways and His thoughts past finding out! Some of the things I wanted to write about in this book could never be calculated or reasoned, but nevertheless, they happened.

Bob told me how he'd always enjoyed my stories. He encouraged me to write them down and said he felt sure that God would help me put it all together. Then, through the afternoon we were talking about a couple of our buddies from Germany, Dr. Michael Peters and Thilo Kramny, who are (as my daughter Haley put it) "probably two of the smartest people we know," and how sometimes they'll travel to the most random places and sites in the world. One such place was Marfa, Texas.

I'd never heard of Marfa, and Texas is one of my favorite places in the world. I asked Bob where it was, and he said, "It's in the middle of nowhere!" I wondered what the attraction was, because Bob told me Michael and Thilo visit every year and will spend an entire week. He went on to tell me how they'd fly in and go to a music store and buy a guitar and a bass, and every night go down to the dining hall of the hotel and entertain and spend hours singing and playing guitars and visiting with these good ole Texas folks.

But the main attraction was the Marfa lights. "You've never heard of the Marfa lights? This is one of the biggest UFO sightings in the entire world! Well, they're not really aliens, but they're definitely *there* and no one can explain why, how, or where they come from!" Of course, this sounded so unusual to me that as the days went by I researched Marfa, Texas, and the sightings of these mysterious lights.

In this book you'll read of things that couldn't be calculated or explained by the scientific mind—yet they happened. And so only a few days after Bob told me about Marfa, my daughter Haley and I were in Texas playing some concerts. "Ironically," we were only a few hours away from this very remote part of the state. So yes, we went to Marfa—and you'd better believe we saw the lights, and they were spectacular and amazing to behold! I'll describe our experience in detail in the next chapter.

So in this book I'll be sharing some stories of our amazing God, but at the end of each chapter I'll also show my favorite Scriptures pertaining to the stories. After all, Psalm 119:105 (KJV) says, "Thy Word is a lamp unto my feet, and a light unto my path."

With all my extensive traveling and busy schedule, I rarely have time to visit with people very much. It seems I'll go in for a concert and do a sound check, get dressed, and then leave shortly after shaking a few hands and possibly signing something for someone. I rarely ever have the opportunity to visit and share my heart. As far as I'm concerned, that's what this book is for.

Let's do something kind of like I'll do with Bob. Let's talk about God, guitars, family, and maybe even little things, like some of my favorite guitars and what strings I use and so on. I'd like to tell you about how I came to meet Christ and what got me into the guitar and who some of my musical influences have been. I hope in some way you'll be "enlightened" and encouraged by reading this book. I know that everybody has their stories to tell. I hope you'll enjoy reading some of mine. —**Doyle Dykes**

Endnote: [1]Taylor Guitars, El Cajon, CA

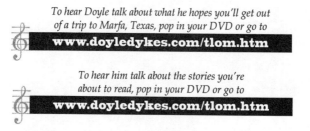

To hear Doyle talk about what he hopes you'll get out of a trip to Marfa, Texas, pop in your DVD or go to
www.doyledykes.com/tlom.htm

To hear him talk about the stories you're about to read, pop in your DVD or go to
www.doyledykes.com/tlom.htm

Doyle's 2002 Taylor
Doyle Dykes Signature Model
Desert Rose Limited

CHAPTER 1

The Lights of Marfa— My Own Personal Experience

Thursday, February 4, 2010. The rain had finally let up in the Big Bend area of West Texas. My daughter Haley and I drove from our good friend Del Way's ranch in Kerrville to find out more about the Marfa lights. We arrived at our hotel in Alpine, Texas, about twenty-five miles away from Marfa and eighteen or nineteen miles from the Marfa lights viewing area. We had dinner and waited until right after sundown, as the lights are seen only at night.

It was cold, in the 20s, but very dry, with wind. The sky looked as if you could reach up and touch the stars. It was a beautiful West Texas night.

We gazed southwest, toward the area where we had been told to look. A radio tower stood in the distance, its beacon flashing. Suddenly we saw lights. They appeared to be car lights, but some were more unusual as one would turn into two and three and then spin in a circular motion. Others at the viewing area saw the spinning lights and thought they couldn't be car lights. Still, we weren't totally convinced. We stayed for well over an hour and then went back to the hotel.

About ten p.m. we went back to the viewing area. More car lights. I decided to investigate and drove into the town of Marfa for the first time. I found it was Highway 67 South that went all the way down to Mexico. We followed the road for about half an hour. We did see lights in the distance, but as we crossed over a hill, they were gone. Strange — but we were still not convinced. Back at the viewing area, I saw what looked to be car lights running downward; and then in a very fast plunge, they were gone. I don't see how any car could've done that. We went back to the hotel and decided to try again before dawn.

Friday morning, February 5, 2010

We went back to the viewing area and stayed over an hour until dawn. No sign of the Marfa lights. Later that day, we did some more investigation. I went to a local music store in Alpine, Texas, as I figured a picker would shoot straight with me. The owner of the store recognized me as he was former owner of the Dallas Guitar Show, which I played at a couple of years back. His name is Mark Pollock and he had moved to Alpine to "retire." He told us he had seen the Marfa lights numerous times. He explained that what he thought we saw the night before were more than likely car lights from

THE VIEWING AREA AT MARFA, TEXAS

THE LIGHTS MAY APPEAR IN VARIOUS COLORS AS THEY SPLIT APART, MELT TOGETHER, DISAPPEAR, AND REAPPEAR.

Highway 67. He advised us to look straight south of the viewing area or to the east, where there were no roads but just thousands of acres of desert: "If you see any lights out there, those would be the Marfa lights." (Take a look at a road atlas. There's nothing there but the desert floor all the way down to Mexico.)

There was a man in the music store named Indio who grew up in that area. We asked if he'd ever seen the lights and he said, raising his voice a little, "Oh, yes, and I said I'd never go back there again . . . and I haven't!" He explained that when was a teenager he and some friends actually went out on the ranch (there was no viewing area then), and the lights appeared, about the size of a basketball or beach ball. Indio said the lights actually herded them up and ran them out of there. "We ran for our lives!"

But Haley and I went back to the viewing area. Highway 67 seemed like a long distance away as it was built up on the foothills. It was hard to believe the lights at night we saw came from there. However, the climate is so dry, and with no light pollution you could also understand how one could see for miles.

We had asked a few local folks around town about the lights. There were some who had seen them and described them in the same way we had read about and seen on the documentary films. Everyone

MARFA MYSTERY LIGHTS

The Marfa Mystery Lights are visible on many clear nights between Marfa and Paisano Pass as one looks towards the Chinati Mountains. The lights may appear in various colors as they move about, split apart, melt together, disappear and reappear.

Robert Reed Ellison, a young cowboy, reported sighting the lights in 1883. He spotted them while tending a herd of cattle and wondered if they were Apache Indian campfires.

Apache Indians believed these eerie lights to be stars dropping to the earth.

Many viewers have theories ranging from scientific to science fiction as they describe their ideas of aliens in UFO's, ranch house lights, St. Elmo's fire, or headlights from vehicles on US 67, the Presidio highway. Some believe the lights are an electrostatic discharge, swamp gases, moonlight shining on veins of mica, of ghosts of Conquistadors searching for gold.

An explanation as to why the lights cannot be located is an unusual phenomenon similar to a miracle, where atmospheric conditions produced by the interaction of cold and warm layers of air bend light so that it can be seen from afar, but not up close.

The mystery of these lights still remains unsolved.

MANY VIEWERS HAVE THEORIES RANGING FROM SCIENTIFIC TO SCIENCE FICTION AS THEY DESCRIBE THEIR IDEAS OF . . .

pretty much described the lights in the same way. They would appear oftentimes as one and then split into two and three, and then they'd even change colors from white to blue and red and so on. They would go into a spinning motion, then dance around randomly and sometimes shoot straight up into the sky.

Others said they'd never even been out to the viewing area. One person said it was just too cold to go out there and then probably not even see anything.

This is just the way some people are about God. They've heard yet they don't really believe or have an interest in seeing for themselves or even take the time to see Him for who HE REALLY IS! In 1 John 1:5 (KJV): "God is light, and in him is no darkness at all." A couple of verses down: "But if we walk in the light, as he

 is in the light, we have fellowship one with another, and the blood of Jesus Christ his Son cleanseth us from all sin."

So now I had just one more person to ask. His name was Roy Cragg, and he was the pastor of the local "Cowboy Church." He said he'd

In a calm yet convincing sort of way he just said, "I believe you're gonna see 'em tonight!"

be glad to meet us at the church, which was on the way back to the viewing area at the edge of town. We got his name from another pastor we met in San Angelo just a few days before. He told us that he had visited with Pastor Roy many times — and he also said he'd seen the lights every time he'd visited there.

When we arrived at the church we had expected a rustic-looking metal-type structure that is typical for cowboy churches, and that's just fine. However, this was a beautiful adobe style building with other annex buildings on site, in the style of a little Western town. Pastor Roy was a very nice man, and you could tell that he was a man of integrity. His answer to me about the lights was that he'd been seeing them as long as he could remember. He said even before there was a Highway 67 people had been seeing the Marfa lights. In fact he told us the Native Americans and the early settlers had spoken about the Marfa lights since the 1800s. He also explained that they seemed to come at random times and under random conditions. "They just seem to show up when they want to," he said.

I gave him some of our recordings and thanked him for his Texas hospitality. Before we left, I said, "Pastor, I'm not out here doing this for my own curiosity" (of course I was curious), "but I'm writing this book that includes stories that just can't be calculated or figured out in the natural." I told him we saw a documentary on the Marfa lights and how a famous Japanese scientist came over to investigate and try to come up with an explanation on the lights. He carried a Buddhist priest with him to "conjure" up the spirits of the lights. I said, "Pastor, if he could do that, then why can't we just agree in the name of Jesus that we'll see the lights tonight? This is our last time to try while we're around here, and I have no idea when we could come back."

In a calm yet convincing sort of way he just said, "I believe you're gonna see 'em tonight!" I knew in my heart he was right.

We got back to the viewing area just as the sun was going down. We looked over to the southwest and sure enough we saw the lights from Highway 67 again. So we concentrated on looking straight south and east of the viewing area platform. Suddenly, Haley spotted the first little dim light. It looked like a twinkling star, very low to the ground and a long distance away. Then the light got brighter and brighter and began to move to the right and then to the left. It changed from a bluish twinkle to more of a yellowish color, sort of like a headlight from an old Model T Ford. Right before our eyes it split off into two, and then to three. Haley once again said, "Dad, over to the left! There are four or five in a row — and now they're changing colors — they're flashing and spinning!" They were clearly visible and it was evident that they were not too far away.

There were possibly a dozen people at the viewing area by then. A family from Fort Stockton, Texas, came up with a pair of binoculars and asked if we wanted to borrow them. It was an amazing sight, to say the least! I could see the lights so clearly, yet nothing or no one was around them! They looked like a huge display of Christmas lights; but suddenly they began to move to the left, then to the right, and then up into the air. The first ones we saw looked as though they were getting closer. It looked to me as though you could see the desert floor lit around the area where they were. Other lights appeared to the southwest—and this time they were clearly not from Highway 67. And more lights appeared in the southeast, but this time much higher than the others. These lights also changed colors and split into two and three and then, suddenly back to one as it would very abruptly move to the right and then down like a meteor and then randomly stop and stay in one spot before completely moving again in the other direction. It was awesome!

I couldn't see how any motorized hobby plane or even a helicopter or airplane or a person or group of people or any other type of vehicle could have done this, and everyone at the viewing stand agreed. We also agreed on the question of why were there only a dozen of us out there and not hundreds or thousands!

So, by now you either think I'm crazy and want your money back, or perhaps you'll read on and see that God is still "pulling the strings." Just as He did when baby Moses's mother put him in the little "ark" or basket by the river and how Pharaoh's daughter found him and, of all things, Pharaoh, the king who had commanded that every Hebrew son be killed, took in the very child that God raised up to destroy Pharaoh's own army, yet Pharaoh raised him as his own grandchild.

I'm convinced that God has a plan for each of our lives. It's up to us if we want to see it come to pass or not. We can surrender to Him and believe His will is the best thing for us, or we can sit around and never even go out to the "viewing area"! Besides, we probably would never see God's will in our lives anyhow, right?

I realize that God's peace and joy, and His love and the miracle of His Grace, are much more miraculous than any mysterious lights in the desert! Although I can't see it or quite understand it, there is no explanation or reasoning for the Grace of God, and yet He has extended this unmerited, unearned favor to us even though we didn't deserve it.

I'm just glad I went out to God's viewing area (the throne of His Grace), purchased by the sacrifice of His Son Jesus and experienced it for myself! He isn't just there randomly, but His light forever shines to all mankind and is available at the mere mention of His name, Jesus!

That cold night on February 5, 2010, I saw the lights of confirmation and direction for this book. I saw The Lights of Marfa.

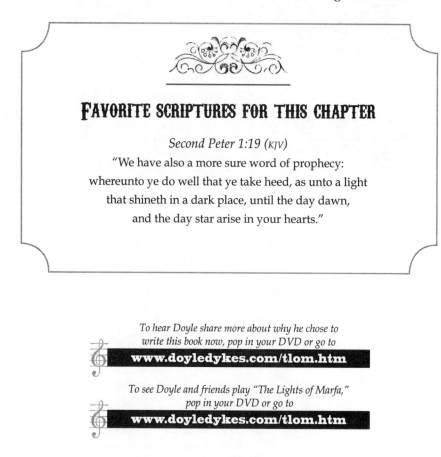

FAVORITE SCRIPTURES FOR THIS CHAPTER

Second Peter 1:19 (KJV)
"We have also a more sure word of prophecy:
whereunto ye do well that ye take heed, as unto a light
that shineth in a dark place, until the day dawn,
and the day star arise in your hearts."

*To hear Doyle share more about why he chose to
write this book now, pop in your DVD or go to*
www.doyledykes.com/tlom.htm

*To see Doyle and friends play "The Lights of Marfa,"
pop in your DVD or go to*
www.doyledykes.com/tlom.htm

*Doyle Deluxe model
(DDX) Taylor guitar*

CHAPTER 2

Why the Guitar, Doyle?

I've been asked this question many times, often on live television and radio shows around the world (secular and Christian). Whether I'm on the *Mark & Brian Show* with Mark Thompson and Brian Phelps at KLOS in Los Angeles (one of the most popular shows in the country), the *Mitch Albom Show* on WJR in Detroit, the *Steve & Johnnie Show* on WGN in Chicago, or a radio station in Shanghai, my answer is always the same. So this is my story.

As a boy I was raised in a Christian environment in my hometown of Jacksonville, Florida. Church was the center of our lives, aside from music. We had church morning and evening on Sunday, prayer meeting on Wednesday nights, and then youth service on Friday nights. The youth service was called Y.P.E. or Young People's Endeavor (how hip!!!!), and everyone young and "otherwise" attended. Also, we had "Revival Meetings" at least once or twice a year that went on every night and sometimes lasted for weeks. Except for the music, which was my favorite part, as far as I was concerned going to church mainly meant missing *Lassie* and Disney on Sunday nights. My grandfather was the choir director at our church for over thirty-three years. I really loved him and would go and help him clean the church on Saturdays as he was also the janitor. They didn't have associate pastors and worship leaders in those days, so that's how he got paid.

AND HERE THEY ARE ... THE BUBBA DYKES FAMILY!
ME, MOM, DAD, AND AUBREY.

Sometimes they'd do really cool things like a passion play at Easter or other drama programs around Christmas and such. I remember my uncle Ronnie Dykes coming over to produce such a play for Easter service. There would be this guy (Brother Udell Jump) propped up on a cross inside the baptistery, and when it came time for the thunder and lightning, Uncle Ronnie would run over and bang on the bass notes of the grand piano with the sustain pedal pushed down, and someone else would sneak up close to Brother Udell with an Instamatic camera and try to get as many flash cubes to go off as they could for the lightning effect. You could hear a lot of clicks from the camera because those flash cubes didn't always work. We'd sit and giggle and then after church we'd all go up to the piano and try to make thunderous sound effects like Uncle Ronnie did. That was pretty cool.

Soon after that my brother, Aubrey, and I would play "Jesus on the cross" at home. It was one of our favorite games for a while. Mom's clotheslines were held up by two T-shaped poles in the backyard and we'd wrap our arms around the top poles. I remember one day telling Aubrey it was his turn to be Jesus and to shut his eyes and pretend he was dead. Then, we normally would take a stick or a broom handle and act like it was a spear and pretend to thrust it in his side, only one time I picked up two handfuls of rotten plums lying on the ground and threw them at him. He proceeded to chase me with a rope when I fell over our homemade go-cart and hit my head on the driveway, giving myself a concussion . . . and that's when I started playing the guitar! HA! Well, not exactly.

In June of 1965 our pastor, Rev. F. L. Braddock, announced that we were having a Summer Revival. This was the time that a little lady named "Minnie" Irene Baxter came to our church to conduct the revival in place of her late husband. She had a presence and persona that communicated well with people, especially the young people. Over fifty young people gave

their hearts to Jesus in her two-week revival. I was one of those people as well as my brother, Aubrey. "Sister" Baxter spoke in such a way that a child could understand. I was eleven years old but I knew in my heart that something was

STICK 'EM UP! WE GOT NEW COWBOY DUDS EVERY CHRISTMAS. THOSE AREN'T EARRINGS IN AUBREY'S EARS...THEY'RE HIS PISTOLS! HEY, CHECK OUT THE TV AND THE STEREO SPEAKERS!

different that summer night in 1965. I remember raising my hands to God and saying, "Lord, if You'll give me a job to do, I'll always tell people about You!"

From that night on I had a desire to play the guitar! So for me, my relationship with Christ and my music go hand in hand. In Proverbs 13:12, "When the desire comes, it is a tree of life." The thing so unusual about this was the fact that I never cared about playing the guitar before that happened. Let me explain . . .

My dad "Bubba" was a singer and a guitar player, and my mother was a singer for "special music" at church (don't know why they called it special . . . it was all pretty special). They would stand my brother and me up in chairs and gather around us and we'd sing four-part harmony around one of those old Shure "Elvis" microphones. (I managed to buy a couple of those old microphones from our church and gave one to my brother, Aubrey, and kept one for my collection.)

I was only four or five when we started singing in front of an audience.

I was only four or five when we started singing in front of an audience. Dad would play his 1952 Gibson Les Paul gold top. I sang bass two octaves high, and my brother sang the lead, and when he was about seven he started taking piano lessons. By the time I started taking lessons two years later, Aubrey was already playing really well. By the time he was ten years old, he was playing in "big church," which was a big deal because we had hundreds of people in our congregation. My dad played the guitar and switched over to electric bass when needed. Our family was known all over as being musicians.

In our house, hardly a day went by that we didn't hear the music of Chet Atkins, Merle Travis, and Les Paul and Mary Ford on the stereo. Dad also loved gospel quartet music so we were always going to singing conventions and gospel concerts. I enjoyed these groups like the Blackwood Brothers, the Statesmen Quartet, and the Stamps Quartet. I had no idea that someday I'd be so involved in that world.

As much as I loved music I didn't want to play the piano at all—especially after listening to my brother play so well. I hated it! One day, I'd had enough. I sneaked up behind him when he was practicing and took a straight pin from Mom's pincushion and loaded it in my little miniature rifle toy that shot tiny plastic bullets. Well, I didn't know it'd really work but it worked perfectly, and the pin stuck right in his behind. He started crying and chased me down the street. He couldn't really

MY BROTHER AUBREY AND ME IN OUR MUSIC ROOM AND THAT WAS MY FIRST GOOD GUITAR...A GIBSON J-45. THIS IS ALSO WHERE I SHOT AUBREY WITH A STRAIGHT PIN USING MY MINIATURE RIFLE.

beat me up but he sure could play that piano! And he still can.

Besides my mother's brother (Uncle Doyle), whom I'll talk about later in this book, I had a friend named Tim Hicks who attended our church and listened to country music and was the first guy who got me interested in it as well. After church on Sunday afternoons, we'd go over to his house and ride his pony and pick guitars together. At one point we had matching Fender Jaguar guitars. This is when I first began listening to singers like Merle Haggard, George Jones, Tammy Wynette, Porter Wagoner, Grandpa

Jones, Roy Clark, Buck Owens, Charlie Pride, and the great pickers who were in the business then, like James Burton on "Working Man Blues" and Grady Martin, Hank Garland, and Harold Bradley.

My friend Timmy lived out on the west side of Jacksonville. That was where all the local Western wear stores were and where the cowboys lived. It was the closest thing to Texas that I ever knew up to that time. That's also the same area where the legendary rock-and-roll bands Lynyrd Skynyrd and 38 Special boys were raised up and first began to play music together. (Years later I would come to know these guys and become close friends with the lead guitarist of 38 Special, Jeff Carlisi. We're good friends to this day.)

Doyle's 1952 Gibson ES-5

One day, my wife, Rita, and I were invited to Allen Collins's home. Allen was one of the lead guitarists for the Lynyrd Skynyrd band. Allen was famous for his great guitar work on their hit "Free Bird." When I got there, all the "boys" came in and just sat on the floor in Allen's living room and listened to me play the tunes of Chet Atkins, Jerry Reed, and Merle Travis, all at their request. I remember the lead singer, Ronnie Van Zant, asking me where I learned to play the guitar. I said, "At church." He asked who I played for and I said, "God."

Then he asked where I would be playing. I invited him to come out to a church where I was playing and Ronnie told me, "Yes, I'd go to church with you anytime . . . and I promise I will but just not tonight. We're practicing for an upcoming tour out at the farm." This was a ninety-nine-acre farm in Green Cove Springs, Florida, a few miles from Jacksonville's west side, with a cabin where they rehearsed and wrote most of their hit songs. It was commonly

ME WITH MY GUITAR PICKIN' PAL TIM HICKS AT OUR CHURCH. HE HAS HIS DAD'S 50'S STRATOCASTER AND I HAVE MY FENDER JAGUAR.

called "Hell House" because there was no air-conditioning. Shortly after this Ronnie and two other band members and a member of the road crew were tragically killed in a plane crash.

Today, there are only two or three of the original band members still living. Ronnie Van Zant and the bassist, Leon Wilkeson, are buried only a few yards away from my father "Bubba" Dykes on the west side of Jacksonville, Florida. Their music still lives on today, and now they're members of the Rock and Roll Hall of Fame.

Neither Timmy nor I ever knew how these times together would pave the way for me later in life to share the stage with the very country entertainers who we would talk about and try to emulate. (I recently shared this story with Charlie Pride at the Grand Ole Opry.) This was the beginning of my love and appreciation for country music.

Tim and I are still close friends. He loves horses and shoots guns and still picks the guitar. He pastors a church in Georgia and is also a deputy sheriff in his town.

Tim's dad also played the guitar at church and had a 1950s Fender Stratocaster, which he would play through an old 1960s

 Fender Bassman amplifier that my dad bought. He once carved an "X" in the back of that guitar with a pocketknife in case anyone broke into the church and stole it. Someone finally did but he was so pleased to be able to replace it with a brand-new 1966 model. Today that old '50s guitar is worth tens of thousands of dollars. (The '66 is also worth quite a bit and Timmy still owns it.) He and his dad were definitely shining lights in the desert floor of my life!

We felt the Lord deserved the best, and our instruments at our church were the best money could buy.

Later, my dad bought a Fender Dual Showman amplifier and donated it to the church. Even though we were raised in a predominantly poor area, none of us knew it! Besides, we felt the Lord deserved the best, and our instruments at our church were the best money could buy.

My first guitar was a thirty-dollar Sears Roebuck Silvertone acoustic. The strings were a little high off the neck, which made it difficult to play. Sometimes Dad would let me play his Gibson Les Paul but most of the time I enjoyed my little Sears. One day I broke one of the tuning keys and would always have to go out to the garage and borrow my dad's pliers and tune the guitar that way.

Then one day my dad saw me walking home from school and pulled up to the curb and asked me to get in the car. He took me to Paulus Music in downtown Jacksonville. As he was speaking with the store owner, I was enthralled with the Vox teardrop-shaped guitars and the Gibson SGs and 335s. When Dad and Fred Paulus, the owner, called me over, they said here's your guitar. I expected to see my little Sears guitar with a repaired tuning key. Instead, they opened the beautiful hardshell case lid to expose a brand-new cherry-red sunburst Gibson J-45 acoustic guitar. That day changed my life. I knew then that my parents had invested in my gift of music and playing the guitar, so that made me really want to practice even more. They believed in me and showed it by purchasing such a nice instrument for me to play. Years later I played a special Taylor Guitars event in that same store with around two hundred people crammed inside. I especially thanked my parents and Mr. Paulus for that day when they enlightened my life, showing me God's direction. I don't believe I would be writing this book if they hadn't done that.

MY BROTHER AUBREY AND ME AROUND 1969. HE WAS PROBABLY A MUCH BETTER MUSICIAN THAN ME BUT I STILL LOOKED A LOT 'COOLER' HOLDING A GUITAR INSTEAD OF AN ACCORDION. AT LEAST I THINK SO!

That taught me a very important lesson: Unless you see the value in something, you'll never invest your time and money into it. One ole fella said to me recently, "Well, I'm not very good . . . I just have an ole cheap guitar." I wanted to say to him, "Maybe that's why you're not so good!" I heard an old proverb: "Anything good not cheap and anything cheap not good!" That's pretty accurate and just plain common sense.

That's why my folks always bought us nice instruments to play—and sacrificed so we could have them. Mom sold Avon cosmetics and had a route that she'd have to work so as to afford the piano lessons. I can't tell you how many hot afternoons in the car after school I'd have to wait on her to deliver her Avon products. I didn't want to take those dumb lessons anyway! A lot of folks smelled and looked nice for no reason, because I didn't learn squat! I hated it with a passion. But the Lord was at work even then because finger-style guitar is very "piano-esque" and much of the technique I use on the guitar I was introduced to on the piano. (Finger-style guitar is playing the bass, chord, rhythm, and melody at the same time—like playing the piano.)

In those early years, I had no idea that one day I would be playing with all of my dad's heroes like Chet, Merle, Les Paul, and Duane Eddy, and even play on the Grand Ole Opry with Grandpa Jones, or travel and record with people like J. D. Sumner and the Stamps Quartet and the Blackwood Brothers Quartet. The thing is, when God puts a desire

THAT'S ME ON THE LEFT SINGING AND PICKIN' WITH MY BROTHER AUBREY. I WAS 2 YEARS OLD AND MAKING UP A SONG..."THE MOUSE RAN IN AND THE KITTY CAME OUT!' I STILL OWN THAT UKULELE TODAY.

in your heart, you'll see things that you never dreamed! It was all part of His plan for my life. And God's not finished with me yet. Or you either! He's still the Potter and we're still the Clay!

I love playing the guitar to this day. It has been my hobby and my passion, and now the guitar to me feels like an old friend. I also love encouraging other people to play music because it's truly a gift from God! That's why there's always more to learn and new songs to write (Psalm 33:3), but the greatest gift is the one who brings purpose to it all . . . Jesus Christ. Again,

THIS IS MY DAD, FRIEND AND GUITAR BUDDY. I BELIEVE EVEN THE LORD REFERS TO HIM AS 'BUBBA DYKES.'

I truly believe He has a "personal plan" for you as well as me. I believe His will is absolutely the best thing for us in this world. I hope you'll be encouraged even more to see God's love and grace in perhaps a little different but meaningful way.

That summer day in 1965 I saw the lights of salvation and a new purpose and desire for my life and since that day, I've never been the same.

To hear Doyle talk about why he loves the guitar, pop in your DVD or go to

www.doyledykes.com/tlom.htm

FAVORITE SCRIPTURES FOR THIS CHAPTER

Jeremiah 29:11
"'For I know the plans I have for you,' says the LORD.
'They are plans for good and not for disaster,
to give you a future and a hope.'" (NLT)

Romans 10:9–10
"If you confess with your mouth the Lord Jesus
and believe in your heart that God has raised Him
from the dead, you will be saved. For with the heart
one believes unto righteousness, and with the mouth
confession is made unto salvation."

Psalm 37:3–5
"Trust in the LORD, and do good;
dwell in the land,
and feed on His faithfulness.
Delight yourself also in the LORD,
and He shall give you
the desires of your heart.
Commit your way
to the LORD, trust also in Him,
and He shall bring it to pass."

Proverbs 13:12
"Hope deferred makes the heart sick,
but when the desire comes,
it is a tree of life."

Proverbs 18:16
"A man's gift makes room for him,
and brings him before great men."

Jeremiah 18:1–6
"The word which came to Jeremiah from the LORD,
saying: 'Arise and go down to the potter's house,
and there I will cause you to hear My words.'
Then I went down to the potter's house,
and there he was, making something at the wheel.
And the vessel that he made of clay was marred
in the hand of the potter; so he made it again into
another vessel, as it seemed good to the potter to make.
Then the word of the LORD came to me, saying:
'O house of Israel, can I not do with you
as this potter?' says the LORD. 'Look, as the
clay is in the potter's hand, so are you
in My hand, O house of Israel!'"

Guitar Stuff . . . Most of the guitars I use on the road
are short scale 24 7/8 inches. I fly them around in the
original Taylor cases with Colorado Case Co.
covers. I use Shubb capos.

SOME OF MY FAVORITE GUITARS ARE

Taylor Doyle Dykes Signature Models. Currently I have the three original
prototypes. I also have the Desert Rose DDSM, The DDSM Nylon,
The DDSM Anniversary, and several working models I use on the road.

A Del Vecchio I got on a missions trip in Brazil and a Del Vecchio copy
designed for Rose Morris, UK, under my pal Robert Wilson.
I bought it at Guitar Guitar, Glasgow, Scotland.

A Gibson L-5CESN (which was a gift from my wife, Rita).

A black Gibson L-4 customized for my dad, "Bubba."
I gave it to him for his seventieth birthday.
Mom gave it back to me after he passed away.

A Gibson Chet Atkins C.E. that was
Chet's personal guitar and his gift to me.

A couple of Gretsch 6120s from the '60s that were
a gift from one of my childhood guitar heroes
Harvey Simmons. I always admired them
when I was a kid going to his barbershop.
Harvey would cut your hair, then sit and
pick you a tune! I also own a 1958 Gretsch 6120.

Three R. Taylor guitars. (6- and 12-string models)

My original 20th Anniversary Taylor . . .
and another 20th, a personal gift from Bob Taylor.
30th Anniversary Taylor Grand Concert

Taylor Electrics (solid body, T-3s, T-5s)

Les Paul 40th Anniversary (signed by Les)

A custom Presentation Taylor Brazilian
(First guitar Taylor ever gave me)

James Burton Tele[1] — a gift from James Burton

A couple of old Fender Telecasters ('50s and '60s)

A very early '50s Gibson ES-5

A Kirk Sand electric nylon string guitar
(Doyle Dykes Laguna Sand model)

STRINGS

GHS[2] . . . always

AMPS

Rivera Sedona[3] and Venus 33. (I have several
Sedona and Sedona lite amps, which are my
signature amps.) Music Man RD 50s and RD 65,
and a 1958 Magnatone amplifier

EFFECTS

Vintage Boss, T-REX, Klon

Ibanez Tube Screamers

Vintage ROSS and MXR

TUNERS

Peterson

Boss and Korg rackmount

T. C. Electronics

GUITAR STRAPS

George Burnham (G&B Leather) in Hendersonville, TN

C. L. Wallis, San Angelo, Texas

Bobby Boyles, El Reno, Oklahoma

FAVORITE BIBLES

King James and New King James

The Guitar Player's edition
(okay, the Amplified Bible . . . HA!)

The Message

GUITAR-PLAYING INFLUENCES (THOSE WHO'VE PASSED AWAY AND THOSE WHO ARE STILL AROUND)

My dad, Bubba Dykes; Chet Atkins, Merle Travis, Duane Eddy,
Hal Kennedy, Jerry Reed, Dwayne Friend, Barry Lackey, Les Paul,
James Burton, Roy Clark, Billy Grammer, Hank Garland, Leon Rhodes,
Jimmy Capps, Lenny Breau, Brian Setzer, and Mason Williams

GUITAR PLAYERS I LISTEN TO

Mark Knopfler, Eric Johnson, Eric Clapton, Tommy Emmanuel,
Phil Keaggy, Caleb Dykes, Billy Gibbons, George Benson, Joe Pass,
Jeff Golub, Martin Taylor, Lee Ritenour, Steve Lukather, Al Dimeola,
Larry Carlton, Duane Eddy, Sonny Landreth,
Jeff Beck, Vince Gill, Steve Wariner, Lincoln Brewster,
Marty Stuart, Warren Haynes, Derek Trucks,
The Edge, Mike Campbell, Jack White, Tommy Allsup,
Rick McRae, Mike Keneally, Jim Nichols, Richard Smith,
John Jorgenson, Barney Kessell, Tal Farlow,
Django Reinhardt, Stevie Ray Vaughn, George Harrison,
Dickey Betts, Brent Mason, Lindsey Buckingham,
Ted Nugent, Darrell Owens, Jeff Carlisi,
Dennis Agajanian, Albert Lee, Peter Frampton,
Lawrence Juber, and James Taylor

Doyle's 2000 Kirk Sand Custom Guitar

OTHER FAVORITE MUSICIANS
I LISTEN TO

Ricky Skaggs, Dave Pomeroy, Andy Leftwich, Rob Ickes,
Paul Franklin, Aubrey Dykes, Jerry Douglas, Ron Block,
Bela Fleck, Tom Keene, Jack White, Chris Thile and the Punch Brothers,
Earl Scruggs, Stuart Duncan, Rick Muchow, the Allman Brothers,
U2, Tom Petty and the Heartbreakers, Union Station,
Emmylou Harris, Wilco, the Beatles, Killers, Fastball,
Tommy Shaw, Ray Benson and Asleep at the Wheel,
Willie Nelson, John Fogerty, Nathan East, Nitty Gritty Dirt Band,
Hannah and McCuen, John McCuen, Delirious, David Crowder,
Brenton Brown, Paul Baloche, and Chris Isaac

Endnotes:
[1]*"Tele" or Telecaster is a registered trademark of the Fender Corporation.*
[2]*GHS Corporation, Battle Creek, MI.*
[3]*Rivera Research and Development, Burbank, CA.*

NEW TAYLOR T-3 GUITAR, NEW ROCKMONT WESTERN SHIRT...
THE GUITAR STRAP AND PICKER...1950'S VINTAGE

CHAPTER 3

Barry the Sailor

I was raised in the port city of Jacksonville, Florida, and where there are major ports, there are oftentimes major naval bases. We had several around Jacksonville, and so we were always having visiting sailors at our church. I'm sure a lot of them came to meet girls, but there were some who were genuine Christians who wanted to worship and have fellowship with us. But they still probably came to meet girls too, which was fine. We met a lot of nice guys back then, and some came, got married, and even stayed around.

I'll never forget the time a young sailor came up to my dad after church and asked if he could play his guitar. Dad wasn't all that inclined to allow strangers to play his beautiful red Gibson 335, but this young fellow seemed harmless—and actually we were curious to hear him play. He took a thumb-pick from his pocket and began to play like Chet Atkins and Merle Travis. It completely blew Dad and me away! He called it "spider-picking"—I called it amazing! It was the first time I ever saw anyone play with their fingers on their picking hand like he did, and he sounded like my guitar heroes! I thought, *Now I get it!* This had to be the way Chet and Merle did it! All that time I'd been trying to play songs like "O by Jingo" and "Blue Belle" with a flat-pick. I

would go home every day and get their records out and try to learn these great songs, and then along comes a sailor who played "Freight Train" just like Chet Atkins. I was blown away! I immediately ran over to my mom and asked if we could have this guy over for dinner. I knew a sailor couldn't pass up a Southern-style home-cooked meal—and I was right.

He sounded like my guitar heroes! I thought, "Now I get it!"

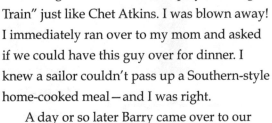

A day or so later Barry came over to our house, and after dinner we had the whole afternoon to play guitars. (That's right, I said dinner. At our house it was breakfast, dinner, and supper . . . and still is at Mom's house!) In one single afternoon Barry changed my life forever. He taught me this simple little right-hand picking pattern that got my fingers working together in the right way, where the thumb played the bass and after-beat rhythm, and three fingers took care of the rest. It took awhile, but before long I was playing Chet Atkins and Merle Travis songs and sounding a whole lot more like they did. I knew that day my life would never be the same. I believe Barry was sent from the Lord!

It wasn't long before Barry was shipped out to sea and we lost touch. I searched for over thirty years for him, but to no avail. It seemed everyone I contacted within our church denomination and any other contacts I made through the years somehow thought that Barry had passed away. I do remember him telling us that he was from the St. Louis, Missouri, area. Finally I took these yellow pads and sheets of paper that I'd saved for years, threw them in the trash, and said, "Lord, if Barry's still around please let him find me . . . I've done everything I know to do."

I felt a real sadness, as if something very dear to me had been taken away — as if someone really had died. This was in April of 2002 — almost a year since Chet Atkins had passed away. All I wanted to do was to honor Barry and thank him for what he'd done for me.

It was the third week of May, about three weeks since I had "thrown Barry away." I was in the Detroit area at Huber & Breese Music store, playing at a Taylor Guitars event. I remember taking a photo with someone with a genuine Liberty Tree guitar, and my daughter Haley ran up to me and said, "Dad, you're not going to BELIEVE who's HERE!" She looked as if she was going to burst. I'd never seen her act this way before.

I turned around and carefully put the guitar on a guitar stand. As I turned back around, there was this gentleman walking up to the stage with a British-style ivy cap and said, "Doyle, I don't know if you remember this but when you were a young boy . . ." and I interrupted and said, "You're Barry Lackey! Well, I've looked for you for over thirty years!" I threw my arms around him and we both hugged and cried and my friends were looking at us wondering what in the world was going on. There were a couple of my friends, Terry Myers and Dave Hager from the Taylor Guitar factory in El Cajon, California, who were there that night for the

BARRY LACKEY, STEVE TURNER (DRUMS), DAVE POMEROY (BASS). AND ME AT CHET ATKINS APPRECIATION SOCIETY CONVENTION. I FINALLY GOT TO HONOR MY FRIEND BARRY IN FRONT OF OVER 1,400 GUITAR PLAYERS.

event. Also, I was very close friends with Paul Huber and Terry Breese and their families who were the cosponsors of the event. When I told them what had just happened, there wasn't a dry eye in the house! I told them I wouldn't even have been there that night or anywhere else playing the guitar had it not been for this man—Barry the Sailor! Terry Myers said to me, "Doyle, you're gonna have to someday write down all these stories you have and put them in a book!"

Well, the rest of the story is even more amazing to me.

Barry proceeded to tell us that he'd quit playing the guitar for over twenty years after a professor at the Bible college he attended told him he should stop playing his guitar because his music was basically a waste of time. He told us that he'd been in bad health and promised God if He'd heal him and let him live that he'd go back to his first love and start playing his guitar for Him. It was only a few weeks before that he went down to his basement and took out his old guitar and could barely squeeze out a chord because his fingers were so weak and out of shape. He decided to just clean it up and put some new strings on it, so he went over to a music store to buy some strings and look at some guitar books and anything that would help him to start playing again.

I love this part. He was looking at the guitar instructional books and came upon a "bargain bin" of books and whatnot. He reached all the

'YOU WOULDN'T BE LOOKING AT THIS PHOTO OR READING THIS BOOK IF IT WASN'T FOR BARRY LACKEY . . . THE SAILOR WHO TOOK AN AFTERNOON OFF AND CHANGED MY LIFE.

way down to the bottom and picked up this book entitled *Top 100 Finger-style Guitarists of 2000* by Mel Bay. He was thumbing through the book when he came to this page that had one of my songs tabbed out and an interview and a photo of me. When he saw my name he thought this couldn't be that kid he visited that day and gave a guitar lesson to! He continued to read the article, and in the interview part they asked me about my main influences and that was when I mentioned Barry. He could hardly believe his eyes. I talked about this sailor who came to our house and in one afternoon taught me more than anyone and how that day my life was forever changed.

When Barry got home that night, he noticed in the book that I played Taylor guitars, so he looked up the Taylor website and there he found a page dedicated to me and the Taylor Guitar events I was scheduled to play. Ironically (as some would say) I was scheduled to play in his area (at Huber & Breese Music Store) and the rest is history! I had no idea he even lived anywhere close to Fraser, Michigan (near Detroit). After the show, I gave him my signature Rivera Sedona amplifier and sent him one of my nicest signature Taylor guitars. He had no excuse not to play now!

When we got in the car that night, we drove several hours. I was so excited about all this there was no way I was going to sleep for a while. I called my parents and said, "You're not going to believe who showed up at our show tonight!" I said, "Dad, who besides you influenced me and actually had more to do with my guitar playing in some ways than even Chet Atkins or Merle Travis?" He and Mom both said at the same time, "That sailor who came over to the house and taught you how to finger-pick!" I said, "That's right—Barry Lackey came to our show tonight!"

For the next few days I spoke with Barry several times and just tried to catch up on things in his life, not only with his music but his wife and family as well. He told me that he regretted not ever getting to personally meet Chet Atkins and how he always wanted to attend the Chet Atkins Appreciation Society Convention in Nashville, Tennessee. I said, "Well I just happen to be playing there in July! How would you like to come down and we'll play something together?"

I'll never forget how he and his wife and other family members came down for the event. I had Jimmy Capps on rhythm guitar, Tom Keene on keyboards from Los Angeles, Dave Pomeroy on bass, and Steve Turner on drums onstage that night. There were 1,400 guitar fans (mostly guitar players) who all rose to their feet when I told our story and honored him that night. It was a night I'll never forget! Later on, Taylor Guitars printed an article about Barry in their *Wood and Steel* newsletter that went to 125,000 guitar pickers around the world. I've also written about Barry in other magazine articles and spoken of him in interviews around the world such as *Acoustic Magazine* in the United Kingdom. I finally got to honor him and thank him for what he'd done for me.

2002 Taylor Liberty Tree Limited. Made from the last surviving Liberty Tree. For the complete story go to www. taylorguitars. com/guitars/ archive/older/ limiteds/liberty/.

We figured it all out together that it had to be the same week if not the very same day that Barry went to that music shop in Grand Blanc, Michigan (which was also going out of business), as I was in Tennessee throwing away all my "Barry Lackey" papers and asked the Lord that if he was still alive that He would let him come to me.

That day Barry saw the "Lights of Marfa" in his own way. There's no way to explain this kind of mysterious yet warm event that happened to two people totally unaware of each other's existence, and how a desire and a prayer brought the light in. Barry and I have played together on numerous occasions and still keep in contact on a regular basis. Even as I'm writing this, he was recently at my concert with his wife, Cheryl, and their granddaughter. I told him about his chapter in this book. He's still playing his guitar! Isn't that illuminating!

The lights of enlightenment and encouragement came to me through Barry when I was a young teenager. Many years later, those lights reappeared to us both. God is Light and in Him is no darkness at all!

Favorite Scriptures for This Chapter

Psalm 33:3
"Sing to Him a new song; play skillfully
[on the strings] with a loud and joyful sound." (AMP)

Matthew 10:42
"And whoever gives one of these little ones only a cup
of cold water in the name of a disciple, assuredly, I say to you,
he shall by no means lose his reward."

Luke 15:9
"And when she has found it, she calls her friends
and neighbors together, saying, 'Rejoice with me,
for I have found the piece which I lost!'"

Doyle's 1995 Taylor Custom
Presentation Brazilian

CHAPTER 4

Ladies and Gentlemen, Elvis Has Left the Building! (And So Did I)

As I mentioned, I grew up listening to gospel music and remember going to the Jacksonville Armory and hearing groups such as The LeFevres, The Rebels Quartet, The Statesmen Quartet, The Blackwood Brothers, The Florida Boys, The Dixie Echoes with Hal Kennedy, The Happy Goodman Family with Dwayne Friend, The Rambos, The Oak Ridge Boys, The Imperials, and many others.

Even in high school, while other kids were into Clapton and Hendrix, I was into Dwayne Friend (guitarist), and besides Chet Atkins and Merle Travis, I loved these gospel quartets. I found in some cases there was more to the story than the clean-cut, spotless lives portrayed by the gifts of these incredible singers, songwriters, and musicians. This is typical when you know how Satan works. His goals are to steal, kill, and destroy, especially anything that has to do with the Gospel of Jesus Christ. Yet, the good part is . . . God's Grace is still truly Amazing!

When my dad took me down to audition for the lead guitarist opening for the Stamps Quartet, I had already made plans previously to go to work with a guy named Smitty Gatlin who was also formerly with the original Oak Ridge Boys. Unfortunately, Smitty passed away in my senior year of high school. I had also just gotten a call from Irby Mandrell, who was the father of Barbara Mandrell; they offered me a job as well. I especially remember one of my favorite musicians and now good friend, Paul Franklin, being her steel guitar player at that time. That would've been such a cool job, but I chose to stay with my gospel roots and go a-pickin' for Jesus!

Doyle's 2003 Taylor Doyle Dykes Signature Model Nylon

The Stamps were at the top of their game in 1972, which was the year I graduated high school. I remember them calling me to see if I could move up a few weeks earlier. I didn't realize it at the time, but they were staying at Elvis Presley's Graceland in Memphis to rehearse for an upcoming record and tour. They had invited me to stay with them there.

I refused, since I was only two weeks away from graduation. The Stamps were the background singers for Elvis at that time. I really wanted to meet Elvis, but I was just as taken with his band members — especially one "Mr. James Burton" on guitar. He was that cool dude who played the pink paisley Fender Telecaster guitar.

My life up to that time was pretty interesting to my classmates. I played in a semiprofessional gospel group called Jack Fowler and the Crusaders. Oftentimes I'd get off the bus and walk right into my class at school, as we would sometimes travel all night to return from our Sunday night concerts.

One Sunday shortly after I had taken the job with the Stamps and was finishing up some dates with Jack Fowler and the Crusaders, we had a random Sunday night off, so I took our drummer, Freddie Mack, and bass player, Ricky Hallman, to my local church. We discussed at first where to go but I kept insisting that we go to "my church," which was the North Jacksonville Church of God. When we got there, we had to peek through the little windows in the doors leading to the sanctuary in order to locate a seat without making too much of a disturbance. The service had already started and I remember one of the guys saying, "Hey, check out the brunette about midways back."I looked and said, "Oh, I know that girl! I've seen her around since Kirby Smith Junior High but actually just formally met her at school about a week ago! She's always been really popular at school. She's been a cheerleader since junior high school. I bet she'll go out with me after church!"

The service had already started and I remember one of the guys saying, "Hey, check out the brunette about midways back."

Ricky just said, "Right, Dykes."

So I stuck around after church to prove them wrong—and to see for myself if she really *would* go out with me. She obviously was way out of my league—but it never hurts to ask, and she sure was purdy!

I remember going up to her and saying, "You want to go out for a Coke?" Now that didn't just mean a "Coca-Cola," but where we're from it was just a generic term for "you wanna go out with me?" The funny thing, Rita loves Coca-Cola more than anyone I know, so I guess my Southern "Casanova" approach was the right one.

She was sitting by her mom, and she agreed to let her go with me. That was it!

After our date I ran home and knelt beside my brother's little twin bed next to mine in our bedroom and woke him up. I started crying. Aubrey asked, "What's the matter?" I told him, "I just met the girl I'm going to marry!" Then he asked, "Then why are you crying?"

I went on to tell him that it was because I just landed the biggest opportunity any young high school graduate could ever dream up, and then I met Rita Moore! We dated until the day I left for Nashville, Tennessee, to join the Stamps Quartet. (There's more to come on that.)

I told him, "I just met the girl I'm going to marry!" Then he asked, "Then why are you crying?"

Before I go any further, I want to tell you a little about Rita. We've been married for thirty-seven years. God gave us four children and now, three grandchildren! She is a private person, and although she's musical herself, she's never made a career out of it. When we met, our attraction for each other actually had nothing to do with music. But she (and her family) are definitely gifted! I've been asked how it works, with her at home and me traveling. Let me tell you, it never gets easier to get up at the crack of dawn, kiss my sleeping wife, and head out. But years ago, as you'll see, she encouraged me to follow the path of ministering through music. And when I'm home, you'd better believe that I treat her as much like a queen as I can afford.

So when I left for Nashville, I had just sold my 1968 Rambler American (so now you know Rita didn't just date me for my car) and my parents drove me up from Florida. My guitar was worth more than my car, but you couldn't drive a guitar to Tennessee! A couple of days later, the band members, office staff, and I were on our way to Waxahachie, Texas, for the Stamps/Blackwood summer singing school. I was to teach guitar lessons at the school. The singers were on their way to New York City and I didn't even see them for about a week after we were in Texas because the guys were recording *Elvis Live at Madison Square Garden*. The album was recorded on a Sunday night and released a week later. It was known as the quickest turnaround for an album to be released.

A few days later the Stamps (singers) finally came to Waxahachie to join the other musicians and me and also to teach vocal lessons at the school. We taught every day so I still didn't see the guys much except for a rehearsal or two before we took off for a short weekend tour and then back to the school for another week of teaching. The Stamps were to play a live show with Elvis in Fort Worth about an hour's drive from Waxahachie the week after.

I couldn't wait to finally get to meet Elvis and his entourage! But that first weekend with the Stamps was not only a marathon on the road (we played in West Virginia, Illinois, and then back to Waxahachie on Monday morning) but a complete emotional roller coaster for me. I was pretty uncomfortable with some things that were going on and just didn't feel I fit in. At the same time, I was critical and stubborn in my attitude. These days I try not to be judgmental, but I'm still stubborn.

To explain what I mean, I need to give you some background on the way I was raised.

I was brought up in a strict household with high moral values (and what's wrong with that, right?). Only thing was, in my opinion if you smoked or drank alcohol at all, you were going straight to the pit! The denomination I grew up in taught total abstinence from alcohol and tobacco. It did not teach us to condemn others for smoking or drinking—but I still did. I had an uncle who pastored a church in a rural area down south. The people would "Amen" him to the heavens when he preached against *using* tobacco. However, once he spoke against *growing* tobacco, he didn't last long at that church!

People are funny. You could grow it because that brought in the grits and gravy, but you were going to hell if you used it! Just so you know, I'm a Southerner and I'm not making fun of Southern folks. That happens to be where tobacco comes from and besides, it's a true story.

I realize the dangers of condemning and passing judgment on others, but I still believe if you're up on a stage or a pulpit and

 are representing Christ, there are some things that are better left alone. I feel strongly about that! Not to be arrogant or self-righteous, but I don't drink alcohol in any form and never have. I have a lot of friends who do and I truly love these folks. Some are businesspeople, some

I still believe if you're up on a stage or a pulpit and are representing Christ, there are some things that are better left alone.

entertainers, some are family members, and others are even involved in ministry.

I do remember on one occasion sitting across the dinner table from a pastor in Europe. He had more drinks than anyone at the table and was actually not at all good at controlling himself. In other words . . . he was pretty tipsy. People came and spoke to me about it as if to say, "What's a minister doing acting like this?" I could have easily approached him and called him a disgrace, but rather I just prayed for him and thanked God for "His" Grace! If it weren't for "HIS" Grace, we'd all be a "DIS" Grace!

Again, I don't mean to condemn anyone, but I simply choose not to have alcohol in my life. You see, my wife, Rita, never knew her father because of alcohol. He walked out on the family when she was only two years old. I do realize this is a terrible problem for some folks and hard to kick, but Rita had two sisters and two brothers! She actually only remembered hearing from her father a couple of times in her life.

Each time was around Christmas—and even then he was drunk. She remembered seeing him for the first time when she was seventeen years old at her grandmother's funeral and it was soon after that he was found dead in his apartment in New Orleans.

Years later, I took Rita and our two little daughters, Heidi and Holli, to Louisiana and found his grave. I'll never forget how she knelt down on his tombstone and brushed away the pine straw with her fingers and then replaced the old faded plastic flowers with a fresh new bouquet. I remember how she was patting her hand on the old gravestone as her tears were falling down and I heard her say, "Daddy, I love you. I'm sorry I never got to know you but Daddy, I forgive you!"

I heard her say, "Daddy, I love you. I'm sorry I never got to know you but Daddy, I forgive you!"

I believe that was the first time I ever really saw forgiveness like that. I had a good father and it was hard for me to relate to those feelings. She called the girls over and said, "Girls, this was your grandpa and my daddy! I wish you could've met him. He was tall and had such a nice voice." That's all she could remember of him. She never told them about the repossession of her Christmas toys because he didn't send them any money because he drank it all away. So, do you think I'm going to bring alcohol into our marriage? I don't think so. Her stepfather was also an alcoholic . . . but that's a whole different story.

One thing for sure, I saw the lights of forgiveness in the most precious way and felt ashamed of myself for holding a grudge against a man I'd never met. I believe forgiveness can unlock heaven for you. I believe it is one of the keys Jesus spoke about to His disciples in Matthew chapter 18. Forgiveness is an action, not a thought. It is the act of releasing someone from a debt or a wrong done against you. It is powerful! It's an action of love and faith.

Now, getting back to the Stamps, the guys treated me nice, and I was stoked about being with one of my favorite gospel bands! These guys were incredible musicians and singers. There was one member of the Stamps in particular who I had a real heartfelt burden for. His name was Donnie Sumner and he was J. D.'s nephew. He was a multitalented individual who not only was the lead singer but was also the arranger for their music, as well as for the vocal backgrounds for the Elvis shows. You can see Donnie in the Elvis documentary films, especially when Elvis would sing gospel music around the piano in their all-night sing-along parties.

Donnie seemed so messed up and running from the Lord; I really wanted to reach out to him and try to help him. The only thing was, he grew up just like me — even in the same denomination. His father was a minister, and he had also gone to Bible college, where he met his wife who was a very strong Christian lady. So I was preaching to the choir. I wondered what I could do to help him! He got real upset with me a couple of times because I made a pretty strong statement about some of his bad habits, but he still treated me kindly. I think it was because he knew how much I cared . . . and that's one of the most important things we can ever convey to anyone. The thing I found out was, these guys really did love the Lord, but when fame, fortune, and a fast-paced life came their way, they got caught up in the middle. I loved these guys and prayed for them every day.

I went to Dallas for the first time when I was with the Stamps. I remember having my first experience eating chips and salsa. I almost cried! I had some packaged up to send to my dad for Father's Day. Although I had traveled quite a bit in my young years, I was never subjected to such different cultures. I was having fun!

Then the day came to go to the Elvis show in Fort Worth. When we arrived at the hotel lobby, we were told that Elvis was resting. Suddenly, his entire entourage entered the room and I was mesmerized by the guy who I'd wanted to meet the most, besides

Elvis . . . and that was Mr. James Burton, Elvis's lead guitarist. I remember how nice and genuine he seemed to be. I've found this so often in the music business. The guys who'd already made it like James didn't seem pretentious and conceited but as nice and friendly as if I'd known them for years. Of course, now I have known him for years and he's just as kind and warm today as he was back then! And the good thing is, James really loves the Lord and gives Him all the credit for his success.

I went to the Elvis show that day with the bass player, Kenny Hicks, and his girlfriend. Kenny and I got along great and he was one hilarious individual. Elvis hired him later as his personal valet. We were also meeting the famous Blackwood Brothers Quartet there as they were also invited by J. D. Sumner to go up and speak with Elvis. Elvis loved gospel quartet music and he was a fan of these guys just like I was!

Doyle's 1980 Handmade Alhambra

And the show itself? I had never seen anything like it. Camera flashes were going off by the thousands creating strobe light effects, and the deafening roar of the crowd was almost at a frenzy stage. I was excited and frightened at the same time because I'd never seen any man get that kind of response and attention from a crowd — and I still haven't. I remember Elvis pulling out a piece of paper with some words written on it and saying, "Here's a new song I hope you'll like. It's called 'Burning Love.'" Such a cool experience and to think I was about to meet this guy!

At the end of the concert, there was the famous announcement, "Ladies and Gentlemen, Elvis has left the building!" And believe me, he had! It was amazing! We scurried out the side door to the Hilton Hotel directly across the street. We pretty much ran to get there, and yet when we did the Blackwoods were already in the room talking to Elvis, and I was escorted to the "green room" and asked to wait for a short while. Then, the Stamps walked in. I'll have to admit, the Stamps were like rock stars, and they treated me like one too. "Hey son, how are you and did you enjoy the show? Glad you're here!" I had finally arrived! Just the fact that I was in this group would open doors for me in the recording field in Nashville as a studio musician — which at the time was what I really wanted to do. I was beginning to enjoy all this.

THIS IS WHEN I FEEL THE CLOSEST TO MY GUITAR AND MUSIC . . . WHEN I'M PLAYING AT HOME.

About that time things started to change. I remember the women who were escorted up and then the party cart appeared, pushed by Elvis's stepbrother, who eventually came to Christ and became a minister. Things were heating up quickly and I was just about to call it quits and leave when one of the Stamps came up and said, "Oh, don't pay any attention to this stuff. Why don't you come down to our private room where you'll be more comfortable?"

I was so thankful, yet I felt something was wrong in my spirit about all this. I remember just keeping to myself, and the Holy Spirit started really convicting me. (Not condemning . . . there's a difference.) Suddenly, it was like He spoke to me directly: "Which King will you play for? Which King will you serve?" I remember saying, *Okay, Lord, just please let me stay long enough to meet Elvis and then I'll make arrangements to leave this group.* He spoke the same thing again, "Which King will you play for? Which King will you serve?" I shut my eyes and suddenly it was like I was in there all alone, yet just a few feet away from the others.

It was like He spoke to me directly: "Which King will you play for? Which King will you serve?"

I remember saying to the Lord, "I promise I'll leave if You'll just let me meet Elvis." Then, I remembered just a few weeks before at my local church when the pastor called me up. All the young folks in the church and my family gathered around me and prayed this prayer: "Lord, please help Doyle! Don't let him go the way of the world . . . protect him physically and spiritually!"

I also remembered a young minister named James Byrd, who was a guest speaker at our church around that time. He warned me in no uncertain terms of the lifestyle and temptations awaiting me. He was the brother-in-law of one of the Stamps and seemed deeply concerned, saying he would be praying for God's protection and guiding hand in my life.

Then, I imagined Elvis the "King" dripping with gold and jewelry on one side and then there was Jesus with His arms stretched out hanging on a cross . . . for me! I realize Jesus called the Holy Spirit "the Comforter" — but let me tell you, sometimes He's not very comfortable, or at least you don't always feel comfortable when you're in His Presence.

I couldn't take it anymore. I was so out of place. I don't know why I said it like this but I stood up in the room and said, "I wasn't raised like this!" They turned around and looked at me like I was crazy. I said, "You think I'm going to be like this and you're wrong!" And so on. I started walking toward the door. They got really angry with me and said some pretty harsh things. They also said, "Man, we've told Elvis about you and stuck our necks out to get you in here!" They told me how Elvis said he wanted to see the guy who took Duke Dumas's (the other guitarist and the one who recommended me) place! "If you walk out of here, we'll see to it that you're blackballed in Nashville! You'll never be able to do anything in the music business again!"

Doyle's 2004 Gibson L5 CESN (a gift from Rita Dykes)

That's kind of scary when you're barely eighteen and all you ever wanted to do was to play with someone like this and record in Nashville. I said something like, "You can call me what you want to, but you can call me gone!"

Kenny the bass player, who had heard all the commotion, ran after me and said, "How are you getting back to Waxahachie?" (Thank You Jesus . . .) I said, "With YOUR car and if you wanna ride, you'd better come now because I have the keys! I'll meet Elvis another time. I'm sure he'll be around for a while!"

Conviction is a funny thing. What seemed totally wrong for me may not have seemed that way at all for someone else! For me, it was a crossroads. You always have the opportunity to act on it or ignore it. I'm not perfect in any sense or form, but I've always tried to be honest with myself and who I am, even in my music. Please don't misunderstand this story. I really loved the Stamps and I loved Elvis. What a singer. As Chet Atkins said, "The boy could sing!"

Very shortly after that, I left the Stamps Quartet. I didn't want to leave the music business necessarily, but for now I'd had enough. I still loved the guys and their music and prayed for them every night, especially Donnie. I literally cried myself to sleep praying for that guy. Even a couple of years later, sometimes I'd get emotional thinking about him and his life and how he needed the Lord.

I moved back to Jacksonville and a year and a half later, I married Rita, just like I knew I would. Pastor F. L. Braddock performed the ceremony. We've been married since 1973, which for a musician is almost as unusual as the Marfa lights! God is good!

Not long after I left the Stamps, Donnie Sumner was hired by Elvis to head up a new group called VOICE. This was to be the ultimate backup group to sing with Elvis along with the Stamps and the Sweet Inspirations and so on, but they also opened the show. These guys pretty much lived at Graceland, or wherever Elvis was, all the time. They said Elvis would stay up all night and sing gospel songs, and these guys were the cream of the crop for him to have around for his own musical enjoyment. I think the gospel in song soothed Elvis's spirit as young David did when he played for King Saul. Donnie Sumner remained with Elvis for a while, until one day he had all he could take. More on that in a moment.

From the Stamps Quartet to Grandpa Jones and the Grand Ole Opry

By now, Rita and I had been married for almost two years. One day she said to me, "Doyle, I think you should be playing your guitar. I believe you're happier when you're playing, and that's what you should be doing." I had worked at a lumber supply company and also for the City of Jacksonville in their engineering department as a land surveyor. Before I became an "Instrument Man," I would often cut line, which was to take a machete and make a path in jungle-like terrain and vegetation. This wasn't very easy on my hands. I would be exhausted and go home with blisters on my hands so bad I could hardly play the guitar.

Once I had to wade across this little black creek. I was about chest-deep in water when a cottonmouth water moccasin (a deadly poisonous snake) started swimming right toward me. When he got about two feet away, he went under the water. I believe that day I was the second guy who walked on water. (Just kidding!)

So I was glad to hear this from my dear wife. Playing the guitar seemed less dangerous. I prayed about it and felt impressed to make a call to Billy Grammer, a Grand Ole Opry star. I'd met him with my folks a few years before. He was good friends with my uncle Doyle (that's right . . . I was named after him) and so he said to me, "Well, if you could play with J. D. Sumner and the Stamps, you could play for any country group!"

To make a long story short, Billy recommended me to Grandpa Jones, the veteran country star. He had been looking for a guitar picker, and a couple of weeks later I got a call from Grandpa Jones's daughter. She also was his agent and asked if I was interested in auditioning to be his lead guitarist. "Ironically" he was performing near our home a week or so later. I was so excited! In fact, when Grandpa came to Florida he said, "I heard you could finger-pick on the guitar like my friend Merle Travis. . . . Can you harmonize too? Do you know any of the old gospel tunes?"

I answered, "Yes-sir!"

"Well, git on up here and pick with us!"

I had already told my boss with the city, Melvin McGregor (who was a huge Grandpa Jones and *Hee Haw* fan), about my opportunity. In fact, he even came to the show and when we got offstage Grandpa looked at me and asked, "Well, do you want the job or not?" I looked at my "other" boss, Mr. McGregor, and he smiled and said, "You have a couple of weeks of vacation. I'll see that you get your checks. Don't even bother to come back to the office unless you left something. I'm proud for you, son!" Timing is everything and honesty is too!

I think Mr. McGregor kept me around so I could pick a little on rainy

GRANDPA JONES AND ME BACKSTAGE AT THE GRAND OLE OPRY IN 1976. AS YOU CAN TELL WE WERE PALS!

days at the office. At least that's what the other guys told me. They all said they knew I'd be out playing my guitar again someday. I still see some of those boys showing up at my concerts.

Once again our local church had prayer for us and we took off to Nashville. My pastor, R. D. Harris, had recommended a church for us to go to in Nashville; his friend Wayne Proctor was pastoring there. A few days later we were already in an apartment and were at church the next Sunday morning. I remember sitting there during the service and looking at this guy directing the singing. He looked like someone I knew.

Sure enough, it was Donnie Sumner! I couldn't believe it. I thought he still worked with Elvis. Donnie was scheduled to sing a special song that morning before the message. I wasn't sure if he even noticed me in the audience but it was Donnie without a doubt. Before he sang he said that there was someone special in the audience he wanted to recognize. It felt as though my heart sort of came up into my throat. His introduction was something like this:

"Not long ago my life was really in a mess and it seemed there was no way out for me. I was on drugs and didn't want to live anymore, even though I was working with the most famous entertainer of all times. I was working with Elvis at the Hilton in Las Vegas and one night I finally had enough. I went up to the top floor of the hotel and walked up to the roof and was about to throw myself off the top of the hotel. I was standing there crying and looking up to God and once more I asked the Lord if there was any hope left for me and if He'd help me and give me another chance, I'd walk away and live for Him.

"Suddenly my mind went back to this young guitar player who had finally landed a good job with a major group (the Stamps) and followed his dream but because

THERE'S STILL A LITTLE 'ROCKABILLY' IN ME THANKS TO ELVIS!

he wouldn't compromise his walk with the Lord, he just walked away. I stepped away from the edge, went back to the elevator, and pushed the Down button to Elvis's floor. I knocked on the door to his bedroom and they let me into his room. Elvis had not been well—in fact, he was already in a hospital bed. I told him I just couldn't do it anymore and resigned right on the spot. Elvis told me he loved me and wished me the best."

We listened in amazement as Donnie also said Elvis told him that he wished he could have left with him and just walk away from it all, but he said that he was too far gone and too many people expected too much from him. Donnie went on to say, "Folks, I just wanted to say that young man I'm talking about is here this morning. I don't know why he's here but I just wanted to say, Doyle—things are okay now and thanks for praying for me, brother!" Then Donnie sang, "It Is Well with My Soul."

I was absolutely flabbergasted! I was crying, Rita was crying, and there was hardly a person who wasn't crying in the building that day. So many people had told me that I'd never make a difference. They were right, I didn't. However, Jesus made all the difference. God had continued to tug on Donnie's heart. I believe He did that for Elvis as well.

Never give up on your loved ones. I have people in my family I pray for every day. Someday I'll get that call or somehow see God's Saving Grace a reality in their lives.

I am a firm believer that prayer changes things and people, and circumstances can change too. I'm sure this was why for so long I would lie awake at night thinking about Donnie and praying for his soul.

On a side note, Donnie was actually the man who hired me with the Stamps. He had the final word. When he resigned shortly after I did to start VOICE, he put a whole new band together. I've always wondered had I stuck around if he would've hired me to play with his band. I already knew what I walked away from leaving the Stamps, but I wondered if I would've had the opportunity to live at

Graceland with the rest of the boys and hang out and record with Elvis and his entourage.

I recently emailed Donnie, asking, just for my own curiosity, if he would've at least considered me for the job. He replied, "I most assuredly would have chosen to have your proficiency supporting our musical effort. I knew that you would have never accepted our lifestyle and chose to not put you in a position in which you would have had to say no." (I love this part . . .) "Getting out was the best thing that ever happened to me . . . not getting in was the best thing that came your way during that time period."

Wow. So now we all know! I also happen to know that Elvis called Donnie a number of times to ask if he'd go back to work for him. He did not.

After being with Grandpa Jones for about a year, I heard the news of Elvis's death. Donnie continues to sing and evangelize and produce records in Nashville. He is one of the kindest and most unselfish people I've ever met. When I was a pastor, Donnie was a regular guest at our church. But now he's an ordained Southern Baptist minister. What's more, he sang backup vocals on my first solo albums and helped produce them. We even recorded a Christmas record together and someday, I hope to record again with Donnie.

As for me and that thing about how I'd never do anything in the music business again? Well, I have and for years I've been a regular guest on the Grand Ole Opry and recorded many albums of my own and traveled the world playing my guitar. And the entire Grandpa Jones experience could be a book of its own. During my time with him, I met people from country music and rock stars to personalities like Carol Channing and Andy Warhol, celebrities who would come backstage to experience meeting others like Grandpa Jones or Minnie Pearl and Roy Acuff. Music is such a powerful tool that thrusts you into a mix of people and events that otherwise would probably never happen. Also, for years now I've been friends with Elvis's guitarist

I previously mentioned, Mr. James Burton. In fact, I've been friends with all of Elvis's guitar pickers — Chet Atkins, Scotty Moore, and Hank Garland as well.

These days I'm still traveling and playing theatres, churches, and festivals, and as I'm writing this, I'm in the process of starting my own television show on a national cable network, which will also be telecast in the UK and different areas of Europe. The show will also have the capabilities of Internet streaming over the Web. One of my first confirmed guests will be Mr. James Burton. I've also asked Donnie Sumner to be on as well. These guys are a blessing to me.

I've seen some extraordinary things and had such great experiences. All I can say is, that night in June of 1972, in Fort Worth, Texas, I saw the lights pointing in two different directions. On one road were the lights of destruction in the disguise of fame and fortune. On the other were the ones I followed, pointing to the

TENNESSEE ERNIE FORD, ME, AND GRANDPA JONES BACKSTAGE AT THE GRAND OLE OPRY. I SANG AND PLAYED WITH THEM THAT NIGHT. MR. FORD SAID I WAS THE 'BEST INTRODUCER OF SONGS HE'D EVER HEARD.'

way of escape and to faith and freedom. In time, my friend Donnie Sumner also saw those same lights — in Las Vegas, the "City of Lights." But this time he followed the ones that led him back home.

FAVORITE SCRIPTURES FOR THIS CHAPTER

Matthew 5:16

"Let your light so shine before men,
that they may see your good works
and glorify your Father in heaven."

Psalm 18:30

"As for God, His way is perfect;
the word of the LORD is proven;
He is a shield to all who trust in Him."

Proverbs 4:18

"But the path of the just
is like the shining sun,
that shines ever brighter
unto the perfect day."

Proverbs 3:6–7

"In all your ways acknowledge Him,
and He shall direct your paths.
Do not be wise in your own eyes;
fear the LORD and depart from evil."

GUITARS AND GEAR I USED WHILE
WITH THE STAMPS QUARTET

A 1968 Gibson L-5 CESN Florentine cutaway

A Kent WahWah pedal
(my very first effects pedal besides an Echoplex)

Fender Twin Reverb with JBL speakers

GUITARS I USED WITH GRANDPA JONES

Gibson L-5 CESN Florentine cutaway

1967 Fender Telecaster

Guild Starfire 3

Les Paul Copy from Greco factory from Japan tour

1939 Martin D-45

Gibson J-45

1960s Fender Twin

*1994–My first Taylor
20th Anniversary
Rosewood*

CHAPTER 5

A Word from an Outlaw

A lot of people never knew that I was a pastor of a small church in Florida. I've been sort of "undercover" for the Lord, I suppose, although I'm certainly not ashamed of that. These were some of the best and most meaningful years of my life. My copastor then was Roy Nail, who is still a pastor to me and confident prayer partner with me to this day.

During this time certain people came into my life who were critical components in what essentially took me to the place where I am today. The funny thing about all that is I didn't have a clue! I was so wrapped up in my little church and was totally enjoying not having to travel, owning a lawn mower, fishing a little . . . whatever I chose. Except for those two years when Rita and I were married right after leaving the Stamps Quartet, I had been traveling since I was in high school, when I was part of The Bubba Dykes Family, and Jack Fowler and the Crusaders, playing in churches. It was good to go home on a Sunday afternoon and enjoy my family.

Don't get me wrong. It was a struggle in a lot of ways. Finances were always an issue. I had a "tent-making" job helping my brother-in-law "Buddy" Tyrrell install shallow wells and sprinkler systems. This was his part-time job as he was also working for

We still had a dirt parking lot but I felt like I was Rick Warren or somebody.

the sheriff's office. Because of Buddy's training, I finally got good enough at this that I had my own jobs here and there. I remember one such job at a business complex in Jacksonville Beach, Florida, owned by a guy named Al Outlaw. He had a wife named Annie who was a fierce, fired-up, feisty evangelist. Annie would go over to Nicaragua and El Salvador or wherever she felt led to go, and preach the gospel even to the military leaders. She could preach, sing, and even write songs. Al and Annie visited our church and heard me play the guitar. They'd also heard my daily radio show, *A Sure Word*, on a local radio station. They asked me to help Annie out with a record, so I produced an album for her. I went from "plumber" to "producer" (in addition to "pastor") with those folks. I called them my "elders at large" since they never really came to our church all the time, but they were definitely members!

Al Outlaw was an unusual fellow as well. In his younger days he ran bootlegged whiskey across state lines and later became a wealthy developer, having actually owned the former Henry Ford Plantation not once but twice in his life. He was no dummy, and neither was Annie. I really loved Annie and Al Outlaw.

I remember the time when we had just finished our little church sanctuary. I was so proud! We still had a dirt parking lot but I felt like I was Rick Warren or somebody. After the building was completed, I felt I could lie back a little and enjoy myself for a while. I'll never forget one Sunday morning worship service when Al and Annie had attended. They seemed to have waited until the crowd sort of died down in order to see me before they left.

Annie said, "Doyle, I was praying for you this week and God gave me a word for you!" Al was standing right behind her and in his sort of gruff and calloused voice said, "Listen to her, Doyle, you know Annie knows how to hear from God!"

She said, "You're not always going to be here pastoring this church. In fact, you're not going to be here long at all. God is about to call you out and you're going to be playing your guitar and ministering to people through your music. In fact, God told me that you were going to be traveling all over the world playing your guitar! You're also going to be 'designing' musical instruments like King David did at the dedication of the Temple in the Old Testament—and you're going to be 'backed' by some of the leading manufacturers of musical instruments and they're going to send you around the world! So there!"

I'm sure I must have looked at Annie like she had three eyes, and I thought, *Hmmm, that's a back-burner thing if I ever heard one.* I didn't know anyone who was a "leading manufacturer," and I was sure they didn't know me either since I was "Internationally Unknown in most countries big and small around the world." I told them thanks and that I loved them, which I did.

It was only a short time later when I really felt the tug to go out and use my musical gifts. I consulted with Annie and Al, but honestly I completely forgot about the "designing musical instruments" thing. But God didn't forget it!

A short while after this conversation, I resigned my position at my church without any scheduled concerts or special music gigs or anything to depend on. My good friend Paul Henson (see "The Old Blue-Eyed Preacher") had asked me to accompany him in a series of meetings he was holding in Trinidad and Tobago, West

Indies. While I was there, I called home and my wife, Rita, had just discovered she was pregnant with our son Caleb—our fourth and youngest. I had left salary, insurance, and even our family doctors. Also, we had made arrangements to move to the Orlando, Florida, area, over two hours south of our home in Jacksonville, for a new ministry opportunity. Things weren't looking too promising for me at that time; however, I had faith and a family who loved me and I loved them and God always took care of us, sometimes miraculously.

I traveled for several years speaking as well as playing concerts in churches. By this time I'd met Chet Atkins, who had given me one of his personal guitars. He told me, "Paul Rivera makes the best new tube amps available today." I had also met guitar innovator and luthier (guitar maker) Wayne Charvel, who had invited me to the NAMM (National Association of Musical Merchandisers) show in southern California. This is the largest music trade show in America and one of the largest in the world. While we were there I recognized the name "Rivera" as we were walking through the trade show floor, and Wayne introduced me to Paul. A year or so afterward, I had just started playing Taylor guitars so I wanted to keep the warmth of the tube sound, so I simply asked Paul Rivera Sr. about the possibilities of building an amp that I could play through from my "Tele" to my Taylor. He said, "You mean build you a tube acoustic amplifier? I'd love to! I don't think anyone has ever done that before. Let's take some time and find just the right speaker combinations and anything else you may want." I told him I wanted a "tube preamp" built in like a studio, and several other ideas that would make this guitar amplifier in a class by itself! This is the Rivera Sedona, which now is not only just an amp but an entire series of amplifiers.

The things Annie had said to me were starting to happen, but I still had forgotten all about her prediction!

A short time after meeting Paul, I met Bob Taylor (see chapter 7), and it wasn't long that he was asking me if I'd be interested in helping him with a certain project. He wanted me to help him design a guitar for stage use that had minimal feedback in the sound system, and that meant experimenting with things such as guitar pickups. This is when I met Lloyd Baggs of the L. R. Baggs Company. I worked relentlessly on this guitar for three years and finally came up with a guitar that I could walk onstage with and not have to "think" about anything but just playing the guitar! It was during that time that I was on the Grand Ole Opry and on national television on the TNN Network and also landed a recording contract with Windham Hill, which was a BMG affiliate label. In other words, my career as a player had finally taken off.

Doyle's 2000 Original Taylor Doyle Dykes Signature Model from NAMM Show

The guys at Taylor figured it was time for my signature guitar, the DDSM. After lots of trips to Lloyd Baggs's (L. R. Baggs Electronics) place in San Luis Obispo, California, and to the Taylor factory in El Cajon working with Bob Taylor and Larry Breedlove, the guitar debuted in January at the NAMM show in Los Angeles. Things were coming together for me—and I'm so thankful it's been on the market for over ten years! Bob Taylor says it's the most "signature" of any signature guitar they'd ever had. A couple of weeks before the DDSM guitar was introduced, I was in Savannah, Georgia, conducting a clinic for Taylor. I had no idea until after the show that Al and Annie Outlaw were in the audience. After the show, I remember them coming up and Annie just looked me right in the eyes and said, "Do you remember what I told you years ago when we went to your church?" (To tell you the truth, I had forgotten what she had told me on that spring day in 1989 standing in our dirt parking lot.) Annie said, "I told you so!"

Then, good ole Al was still saying, "Yeah, I remember Annie telling you all this . . . I told you she knows how to hear from God!"

That was the last time I ever saw Al, as he's now with the Lord. I'll never forget these two as they were the nicest "Outlaws" I'd ever met.

Since that time at my church, I've been around the world and have indeed been "backed" or supported by some of the leading manufacturers in the music industry! I've worked with Bob Taylor to develop his short-scale guitars as well as two different types of signature guitar strings with the GHS Corporation. I continue to search for new innovations that perhaps will help people — including me — to play and sound better. I also try to encourage others to play and use their gifts to bless others. I'm blessed to continue to promote these companies who have been so good to me and who have genuinely made a difference in music.

People who are keen to listen and obey God are sometimes the ones you least expect it from and sometimes at a time when you least expect to hear it! All I know is that I saw the lights of confirmation, foresight, and encouragement from an "Outlaw" named Annie . . . and it changed my life!

Favorite Scriptures for This Chapter

Proverbs 8:12
"I, wisdom dwell with prudence,
and find out knowledge of witty inventions." (KJV)

First Chronicles 16:33 (KJV)
"Then shall the trees of the wood
sing out at the presence of the LORD,
because he cometh to judge the earth."

Ephesians 3:20–21
"Now to Him Who, by (in consequence of)
the [action of His] power that is at work within us,
is able to [carry out His purpose and] do
superabundantly, far over and above all that we
[dare] ask or think [infinitely beyond our highest prayers,
desires, thoughts, hopes, or dreams]—
To Him be glory in the church and
in Christ Jesus throughout all generations
forever and ever. Amen (so be it)." (AMP)

1994–My first Taylor
20th Anniversary Rosewood

CHAPTER 6

Blue Lights Flashing

A number of years had gone by since the Outlaws had spoken to me. In fact, I had completely forgotten about all that. It felt as if no change had taken place in my career, nor had I experienced any great blessing or return for being gone almost constantly, trying to supply my family's needs as well as share my music and message with the world. I was tired and frustrated.

I specifically remember one spring morning in 1991. I had only been home one day in an entire month and was just returning from Savannah, Georgia, only to repack and leave again for California. I literally ached to stay home with my family but I couldn't afford it. I had been praying for direction for my life. I was anxious and didn't feel the Peace of God that keeps our hearts and minds in Christ Jesus (Philippians 4:6–8). We'd moved around a lot, and here I was traveling all the time. Nothing seemed to be working. I didn't even have the money for a plane ticket, so I loaded my guitars in my van and headed out of Nashville for the central valley of California.

It was a cold and foggy morning as I left home about 5:00 a.m. I was alone and remember praying that morning for strength. In fact, I always spent the first hour or two in prayer even though I was driving. This particular morning was probably the worst I'd had in a long time. I stopped to get a cup of coffee a few miles between Jackson and Memphis, Tennessee. I was trying to pull myself together because I felt so tired and homesick that I thought I was going to have to go back home.

GOD'S STRENGTH TRULY IS MADE PERFECT WHEN WE FEEL OUR WEAKEST.

I had never felt so insecure. I began to weep. "Lord, if You don't help me right now, I'm going back home! I can't do this anymore. Nothing's happening for me and I don't want to leave my family. I don't have the strength anymore."

As I was about to turn around at the next exit, I saw the sky flashing blue. I looked in my rearview mirror and saw a Tennessee state trooper trying to pull me over. It was so foggy I took the next exit as I was going to anyway and make a U-turn back home. I remember him coming up to my window and saying, "Okay, license and registration!" Then he asked me to get out of the van and go around and open up the doors so he could look in. My guitars and suitcases were piled everywhere as I had just thrown everything in to leave early that morning. I was also carrying an extra guitar or two because I needed to record a new "cassette" so I could have something to sell at my concerts. I had purchased a small multitrack recording deck and took it as well and had planned to set it up at a friend's home and record on the nights I wasn't performing. I had been writing and getting ready for this but although I lived in Nashville, I couldn't even afford to go into a studio to record. This was all such a change from years earlier when I was recording in some of the best studios in Nashville. I was ashamed and felt like a failure.

As I turned to shut the door, a tear fell down from my face and onto my jeans. The state trooper saw it and looked at me and asked me what was wrong.

The state trooper saw all this and asked, "Is all this stuff yours?" I answered yes and that I was a musician and played in churches. Then he told me to get into the front seat of his police car. I did my best not to show it, but all this time I still had tears in my eyes. Although the state trooper had nothing to do with my being upset, he wasn't helping the situation at all. He said to me, "Shut that door if you don't mind, it's a little cold in here." I thought, *Sir, you have no idea*, but I didn't say that.

As I turned to shut the door, a tear fell down from my face and onto my jeans. The state trooper saw it and looked at me and asked me what was wrong. I felt a lump in my throat the size of an orange and honestly could not talk. I did manage to say, "I'm sorry." He said, "What'd you say?" I could hardly talk so I said, "I'm sorry," again and he asked me what was wrong.

I just kept looking down and wiping tears from my face. I was thinking how I felt lower than I'd ever felt in my life and had been asking God for help and now here I was sitting in a police car. I guess I could've said, "Thanks a lot, Lord! I was hoping for maybe an angel or something and got pulled over by a TENNESSEE STATE TROOPER! Next thing you know I'll be a jailbird!"

Actually, I wasn't even up to thinking like that. I was totally at the end of my road. Or at least I thought I was.

Then the state trooper said, "Quit saying you're sorry! Didn't you tell me you played in churches and stuff?" I nodded.

"Well then, you're anything but sorry — you're a man of God!" Then he asked, "Sir, do you have a family?" I nodded again.

"Is everything okay at home?"

When he said that I turned and looked him in the face and said, "Yes sir, and that's the problem. I have a wonderful wife and four children and I didn't want to leave again because I've been gone so much lately." Then I added, "Sir, I think I'm exhausted." He asked me where I was going. I told him I was going to California, and so help me, he said, "Did God tell you to go to California?"

"Sir?"

He asked me again, "Did God tell you to go to California?"

You see, another reason for my going that far was also to search for direction and an answer. I was planning on spending a couple of days fasting and praying for direction. I felt like anything but a man of God right then, but I looked at him eyeball to eyeball and said, "Yes sir, I believe He did!" He said, "Then you're gonna make it!" (Except it sounded more like, "Then you gone make it)

I can't explain how incredibly comforting he sounded as he spoke to me. It was like I knew him! He seemed like someone I'd gone to church with growing up or something. He went on to tell me how he also had a family in east Tennessee and how they'd transferred him to west Tennessee and how he hadn't seen his family in several weeks. He said, "Sir, I know how it is to be away from your family and that's tough on any man!"

He looked at me with my license and registration in his hand and gave them back to me and said, "Sir, here's your license and registration . . . now I do encourage you to slow down a little because it's really foggy out this morning. But you know, I can see now that I didn't pull you over for that anyway; I pulled you over to encourage you. I'm a state trooper but I'm also a Christian and I pray in this police car every day. Sir, I want you to know that I'll be praying for you every day. How long will you be gone?"

I answered him, about three weeks. He said, "Sir, I want you to know that for the next three weeks you have a friend, a state trooper who will be praying for you. Now I'm telling you, you're gonna make it and not only are you gonna make it, but I believe you're gonna have the best trip you've ever had and God's gonna do some great things out there in California!"

I sat there completely amazed. I asked him if I could give him some of my cassettes to listen to as I couldn't afford to make a CD yet. I loaded him down with everything I had ever recorded and went on my way. I remember thinking that maybe God really did send an angel. I looked back to see if he was still there and SURE ENOUGH—he was. (HA!) He may not have been an angel, but he certainly did the job of an angel that day. This reminds me of the Scripture in Matthew 5:16: "Let your light so shine out before men, that they may see your good works and glorify your Father in heaven."

The light of encouragement shined on me that day.
I did go to California and prayed and fasted for direction and even got some recording done. I'd also like to mention that I had some dear friends out there who encouraged me and helped me get through this time in my life. Just to name a few, they were Jim Coker and his wife, Jackie, and Darrell and Barbara Owens. Not only did these folks help me to continue working in California but

they also helped me in my music. Another is Kirk Sand in Laguna Beach who also builds fine guitars. I'm grateful for these folks and will never forget them.

My pastor friend Doug Young in the Palm Springs area actually told me how he believed one day I'd be writing a book. I remember looking down at the desert sand and shaking my head and wondering why he was saying all this to me. He said one day it would happen: "God will send people your way to encourage you when you need it the most."

Perhaps this is why I'm sitting here writing this to you. It's my turn to say, "You're gonna make it!"

So, that trip to California was indeed a turning point. However, it was when I came home that I began to see the lights of change! When I returned home I was restless and still on California time (Pacific). It was about two or three o'clock in the morning. We had a room over the garage that was sort of a family/playroom area. I went in there and had a good talk with the Lord about things. I was still a bit frustrated and began to talk to God just like I'd talk to a friend or family member. In fact I said to Him, *Lord, please tell me what to do. You know I'll go wherever You tell me and do whatever You want me to do; just please tell me! I need direction!*

I don't say this much, but I believe God spoke to me then. In fact, I know He did. Jesus said, "My sheep hear My voice and I know them." I truly believe He said to me, "You tell Me what YOU want!" I've always used the Scripture in Psalm 37:4: "Delight yourselves in Him and He will give you the desires of your heart."

I believe, to be literal, that God does give us the desires of our hearts. In other words, He'll give you desires you never thought you'd have. That's why some people leave their careers and go into the mission field and so on. My minister friend Paul Henson once told me that he believes that God (more often than not) directs us through our own desires, and how it's not unusual for the things you've always wished for and dreamed about to be the very thing, that God intended for you—because He's the one who put the desire there in the first place.

The cool thing about this is Psalm 37, verse 5 goes on to say that if we would commit all these things to Him, then He will bring them to pass! I think that's a pretty good deal! Don't you?

So I said, "Lord, I don't want to be an evangelist anymore and preach as I have before, but I want to be a musician again. I want to see my Grand Ole Opry friends and be a part of that world again. I miss seeing people like Porter Wagoner in his rhinestone suits and I'd like to wear boots and Western suits if I want to and not feel funny about it. You know I've always loved that kind of thing. I want to reach musicians for Christ and tell them they don't have to be on drugs or alcohol or some other substance to be creative. I want to influence other musicians to turn their gifts back toward You because YOU GAVE US THE GIFT OF LIFE AND MUSIC!"

I felt as if something was being pulled out of me and something was being pushed into me at the same time.

When I said that, it was like heaven came into the room! It's hard to explain, but I felt as if something was being pulled out of me and something was being pushed into me at the same time. I felt it was a miracle taking place. And it was! It wasn't long after that I found myself back in California and met the great luthier Wayne Charvel and amp designer Paul Rivera, as well as Kirk Sand. Soon the whole Taylor Guitars thing took shape, and through that, I've been in front of thousands of musicians pretty much every week for the last fifteen years. I've always asked God to help me to represent the music dealers, promoters, record business people, and the companies that sponsor me as well and professionally as

I can, but that I would also represent Him well as He truly is the GIVER OF LIFE AND MUSIC. I've seen local musicians, soldiers, policemen, firefighters, doctors, ministers, teenagers, old folks, moms, dads, and even famous musicians and movie stars with tears running down their faces because they felt something that perhaps they'd never felt before and that was the power and the presence of God. He's our Heavenly Father and you can feel that He loves us! This is what many say is "the Anointing" — or you could say, God shows up!

It's amazing how this all goes back to when I was an eleven-year-old kid and found salvation and a job to do, which was to play the guitar and tell people about Him — but sometimes, we all need the lights of encouragement and direction. If you seek, you'll find, and if you knock, the door will be opened, but if you waver, you're like a wave tossed to and fro (Matthew 7:7; James 1:5–8). Isn't it wonderful to know God knows the difference between our wavering and our just being tired and needing encouragement! As the Marfa lights seem to come at random times, God sometimes seems to "show up" randomly as well — perhaps even in the form of actual lights themselves like "Blue Lights Flashing."

Doyle's 2000 Kirk Sand Custom Guitar

Favorite Scriptures for This Chapter

Galatians 6:9

"And let us not grow weary while doing good,
for in due season we shall reap if we do not lose heart."

Matthew 11:28

"Come to Me, all you who labor and are
heavy laden, and I will give you rest."

Psalm 37:3–5

"Trust in the LORD, and do good;
dwell in the land, and feed on His faithfulness.
Delight yourself also in the LORD,
and He shall give you the desires of your heart.
Commit your way to the LORD, trust also in Him,
and He shall bring it to pass."

Proverbs 16:3, 7, 9

"Commit your works to the LORD,
and your thoughts will be established. . . .
When a man's ways please the LORD,
he makes even his enemies to be at peace with him. . . .
A man's heart plans his way,
but the LORD directs his steps."

Doyle's 2002 Taylor
Doyle Dykes Signature Model
Desert Rose Limited

CHAPTER 7

Taylor Guitars— The Complete Story

As I've already said, when I was pastoring Day Star Church on the outskirts of Jacksonville, I knew I was going to leave and go back into traveling and playing music again. Annie Outlaw was right. I wasn't going to be there long. In fact, I already knew that in my heart.

When I finally got the "go-ahead" in my spirit to make the move from my pastorate to a full-time music career, as well as having counseled with my family and my good friend and copastor Roy Nail (who I still work with), I started setting things in order to resign. I sold everything I had and put everything back to the church so as to leave on good terms and not leave the church with a lingering debt. The only thing left that we owed was ten thousand dollars on an air-conditioning system. Everything else was pretty much debt free.

At this time the Greater Jacksonville Fair was bringing in Roy Clark and his band as part of the entertainment for their huge annual event. I contacted some friends who were helping to promote the concert and asked if I could get in to see Roy. My uncle Doyle (whom I was named after and who was nicknamed "Smitty"

WGN'S STEVE KING AND JOHNNIE PUTMAN AND ME IN CHICAGO. (2004)

Smith) knew him long ago and would write us and tell us about Roy being on *The Beverly Hillbillies* and such things before the public would actually see the show. I found out that Roy really loved my uncle — which I understood because I loved him as well!

Uncle Doyle was a huge influence on me and on my personality, character, and persona. I still keep photos of him in his Western suits in my studio. He was one of the most talented people I've ever met, even to this day!

While I was traveling with Grandpa Jones, we played the Smith- sonian Institution in Washington, D.C., where my uncle Doyle lived. We were playing a special show honoring Grandpa as a national treasure, and because it was basically billed as American folk music, I was asked to play the show acoustically. I didn't have a decent guitar for that, so Uncle Doyle loaned me his 1939 prewar Martin D-45.

He told me that night that the only fellow he ever allowed to borrow that guitar was Roy Clark the night he played Madison

Square Garden in New York City. My friend Billy Grammer, who recommended me for the job with Grandpa, also knew Roy, Uncle Doyle, and that old Martin. Billy told me a story how he and my uncle Doyle had taken a short break and walked outside between sets at a nightclub where they were performing, when suddenly people were pouring out of the club because it had caught on fire. Without hesitation my uncle ran back inside the burning building, risking his own life to save the old 1939 D-45 Martin guitar. So you see, this guitar had a history and a lot of love around it. Uncle Doyle reemphasized the fact that the old Martin would someday belong to me, but that wasn't in my thoughts since I wanted my uncle around forever!

"Boomerang" DDSM made from Bob Taylor's private wood stock. Doyle's favorite guitar. In late 2010 he gave it to a church to raise funds (which is why he signed the headstock). When a group of friends found out, they bought it back and returned it as a Christmas gift.

Sadly enough, Uncle Doyle passed away unexpectedly a short time later. I got calls from folks like Billy Grammer of course, and Beaudloux and Felice Bryant, who were also great friends and admirers of Uncle Doyle. They were songwriters and had written "Bye, Bye Love" and "All I Have to Do Is Dream" for the Everly Brothers, as well as "Rocky Top" and many country and pop music hits of the day. Most people that spoke to me also mentioned how "Smitty" loved me and wanted me to have his old Martin D-45 guitar.

When I went to see Roy at his show in Jacksonville, I carried the old Martin with me. People were whispering things like, "Look at that guy coming back here trying to sell

ROY CLARK AND ME WHEN I GAVE HIM THE OLD MARTIN

Roy Clark a guitar — who does he think he is!" A few minutes later they were taking pictures of Roy and me as I had just given him the guitar. I remember saying to him, "Roy, I'm a minister and a musician and I've given away instruments to some of the poorest people in the world through our ministry (we called it 'Music for Missions'), but sometimes I believe the Lord wants even the most successful and popular people to know how much He loves them too!"

I found that when there's a need that's "Big" . . . I needed to give "Big."

He looked at me with tear-filled eyes and said, "I know this guitar! This was Smitty's!" And I told him who I was and how I traveled with his old friend Grandpa Jones a few years before. He remembered my name but we never got to know one another — even though I had been invited to some Clark family "pickins" over at the old Sho-Bud steel guitar store and factory by Mr. Shot Jackson himself, who also played in Roy's family band. I was always gone or busy and never had the opportunity to go sit in. (Recently I've been in contact with Roy and he told me he still has the guitar. We've planned to meet and spend some time together even as I'm writing this story.)

I found that when there's a need that's "Big" . . . I needed to give "Big," and that was the biggest and most treasured thing I owned. It was worth considerably more than the debt at the church, but when the final day came and I left, the debt was paid in full from an outside source. Something else I learned: you reap *what* you sow, and not necessarily *where* you sow! If you give to someone, don't expect anything back from them, but you can indeed expect a return blessing. I typically don't talk about it when I give, as I believe my reward in heaven is greater than anything we can get in return here. However, the law of sowing and reaping that was given to man since the beginning of time also includes your life now on earth (as it is in heaven). There is a season of time in all this as in my case, and the greater blessing was yet to come!

A lot of so-called acoustic music bored me and it just seemed so foreign to my personal taste.

As much as I loved Uncle Doyle's old Martin guitar, I didn't play it very well. I've had some great guitars but nothing to compare with that old guitar. They call the prewar Martin D-45 the "Holy Grail" of acoustic guitars. I had the best and felt like I sounded the worst when I played it. The strings hurt my fingers and it, along with other acoustic guitars I'd played, made me feel like I would never be an acoustic guitar player. Plus, a lot of so-called acoustic music bored me and it just seemed so foreign to my personal taste.

But that was about to change.

Wayne Charvel

As the years went by I found myself playing at a small church in Paradise, California, with pastors Steve and Sandy Grandy. Pastor Steve introduced me to a guy in his church who, as he put it, "built guitars for a lot of famous people." Well, I'll have to say he wasn't exaggerating in the least, as this man was Wayne Charvel, who had built guitars and even contributed to the careers of artists such as Eddie Van Halen and Billy Gibbons of ZZ Top, and started a whole new revolution in the guitar industry with the "Super Strat," which was a more modern-style guitar designed mainly for rock and metal musicians. Wayne had invited me to breakfast the next morning before I left town and asked if I would play his guitars at the next NAMM Show. He also suggested that I play an acoustic guitar — namely, a Taylor guitar. I'd never even heard of Taylor before but sort of went along with his suggestion, to be nice.

Some months later at the 1994 trade show, I played for his booth. The business was called W.R.C. Guitars. At the show Wayne also introduced me to Paul Rivera, who became a fierce friend and business partner in our Sedona and Doyle Dykes Signature model amplifiers. He also introduced me to Johnny Davis of Barcus Berry Pickups as well as John McClaren of GnL Guitars, with whom I've had a great relationship for years. Every time we went

I DON'T PLAY A TAYLOR BECAUSE I PLAY ACOUSTIC GUITAR, I PLAY ACOUSTIC GUITAR BECAUSE OF TAYLOR.

by the Taylor Guitars booth, Wayne's contact person was away and he hadn't met Bob Taylor himself, so we just left.

A month or so after the NAMM show, I felt impressed to go back to California where all of these companies are based and follow up on these new contacts. I actually cancelled a trip to Ireland to do this. I went over to Rivera Research and Development, and Paul Rivera immediately set me up with an endorsement deal. When I called Johnny Davis at Barcus Berry Pickups, he asked how I liked my new pickup he had given me at the show. I told him I didn't know because "I didn't have an acoustic guitar to go around it!" He laughed and suggested that I get a Taylor guitar. He explained how he and Wayne Charvel had spoken about it and he offered to take me down to the factory to play one. I reluctantly agreed since I really didn't think I would be playing their guitars very much. As I explained previously, I just didn't feel the acoustic guitar was for me. When Johnny Davis drove me down to El Cajon to the Taylor factory, I almost felt I was wasting a day. I had only a short time to spend in Southern California and was more interested in playing electric guitar anyway. But I thought, *How bad could it be?* I just decided to go and have fun and enjoy my time with my new friend Johnny.

There was a fellow at the factory who took us around and showed us the Taylor operation, which was very nice but at that time also pretty small compared to what it is today. I was blown away with the fact that they also built their own guitar cases, but I'll never forget that first Taylor guitar they placed in my hands. I almost cried! (It was like my first Tex-Mex chips and salsa experience all over again!) I never knew an acoustic guitar could play so easy and sound so good!

About that time, Bob Taylor walked in. He was also very busy that day and really didn't have time to stop and meet another guitar player since he was trying to build guitars and run a factory. They asked me to play a couple of songs for Bob and then Bob asked me to play for his partner, Kurt Listug. They took me into their conference room and their vice president and artist relations guy, T. J. Baden, also came to hear me play. I played some fast things like "Zaccheus" (which I wrote in the '70s when I was with Grandpa Jones) and some Jerry Reed and Chet Atkins stuff.

I didn't know any of these people, so I decided to just be myself and play some worship songs. I started playing some of the old hymns such as "What a Friend," "My Jesus I Love Thee," and "The Lord's Prayer," and I heard someone humming along. Then I played some of the more current worship and gospel songs such as "On Holy Ground" and "Sing Hallelujah to the Lord," and again I heard humming.

It seemed the more I'd play, the more I'd hear someone humming. Who was that?

It was Bob Taylor. There was a connection between the two of us that has remained strong to this day. Also, I felt a camaraderie with T. J. and Kurt as well and just knew I was home. Johnny Davis did too! They told me they'd like for me to play their guitars, but at that time I couldn't even afford a set of strings. They sent me a loaner until I sold my old vintage Gibson L-5 CES guitar, and then I bought two Taylors, one for me and one for my daughter Holli for her sixteenth birthday. The rest of the money went on the down payment for the home we were purchasing. All things do work together for good!

I have played hundreds of Taylor events around the world for thousands of guitar players. I love talking about guitars and encouraging others to go out and do the same. As I said earlier in this book, my father, "Bubba," always owned nice guitars and encouraged me to do likewise. Unless you see the value in something, you'll never invest in it! I try to encourage folks to see the intrinsic value of music as coming from the inside, being inspired and heartfelt and all that, but it's also important to find a great instrument to express it on. It makes it better for the player and especially for the listener.

Taylor changed my whole style of playing and the way I approach music. The dynamics and the clarity, as well as the versatility of the acoustic guitar and the ease of playing, moved me to write new songs and even play differently. People took notice. I was on the Grand Ole Opry again. I've seen places I never dreamed and performed in famous venues such as the Cavern Club in Liverpool, the Florida Theatre (which was a big deal to a Florida kid), Angel Stadium and Harvest Church with Greg Laurie, the Savoy Hotel in London, the Wiltern Theatre in Los Angeles, and the Slack-key Festival in Honolulu, Hawaii, the Yamaha Music Center in Tokyo, Japan, Saddleback Church with Rick Warren—just to name a few. I've contributed columns to guitar magazines and been featured in practically every music magazine imaginable in America as well as Europe, Asia, and Australia. I've appeared on national television and many national broadcasts on radio. What I'm trying to say is, I've found my niche through the acoustic guitar and I owe so much of that to Taylor Guitars. I don't play a Taylor because I play the acoustic guitar, but I play the acoustic guitar because of Taylor! This is not a commercial but just an example of how the "LIGHTS" came on in my life. No one ever paid any attention to me and my music until I started playing it on the acoustic guitar. Isn't that amazing?

What's also amazing is I'm convinced it all started through giving. Honestly, after giving the old Martin away and now being involved enough with Taylor that I would never have to buy another personal guitar (even though I do because I love guitars), doesn't it make sense to say that the night I gave Roy that guitar, I saw the lights illuminating the law of sowing and reaping as well as building a foundation and a vehicle that literally has been a light that has shown around the world! In other words . . . it's a God thing!

After the experience with Roy Clark and the vintage Martin guitar in 1989, I encountered an illumination of faith that was the substance of the things I had hoped for and also the evidence of the things I was yet to see. And now there's much I have seen—and the lights haven't gone out yet!

Think of it this way: seeds grow and get their energy from the sun—in other words, light! Seedtime and harvest is a law. You reap what you sow. This even started in Genesis 1:11–12.

After meeting Bob Taylor, I've seen the lights of the sunsets on many foreign lands . . . I've encountered the lights of encouragement on the faces of people of many cultures . . . I've seen the lights of friendship and faith shine brightly even through hardships of my own . . . I've seen the stage lights of the Grand Ole Opry again and many other bright spots in my life. I've seen the lights of blessing to my family and the lights of friendship with people otherwise unknown to me. I've seen the lights of sowing and reaping, and the harvest is sweet!

SOMETIMES WHEN I'M PLAYING THE GUITAR I CAN SHUT MY EYES AND FEEL THAT I'M STANDING IN A PLACE LIKE THIS. THAT'S WHAT MUSIC DOES TO ME.

FAVORITE SCRIPTURES FOR THIS CHAPTER

Hebrews 11:1
"Now faith is the substance of things hoped for,
the evidence of things not seen."

Second Corinthians 9:6
"But this I say: He who sows sparingly will also reap sparingly,
and he who sows bountifully will also reap bountifully."

Galatians 6:7
"Do not be deceived, God is not mocked;
for whatever a man sows, that he will also reap."

Luke 6:38
"Give, and it will be given to you: good measure, pressed down,
shaken together, and running over will be put into your bosom. For with
the same measure that you use, it will be measured back to you."

Ephesians 3:20–21
"Now to Him Who, by (in consequence of) the [action of His] power
that is at work within us, is able to [carry out His purpose and]
do superabundantly, far over and above all that we [dare] ask or think
[infinitely beyond our highest prayers, desires, thoughts,
hopes, or dreams] — To Him be glory in the church and
in Christ Jesus throughout all generations forever
and ever. Amen (so be it)." (AMP)

Doyle's 2002 Taylor
Doyle Dykes Signature Model

CHAPTER 8

White Rose for Heidi

In 2000, at the NAMM trade show in Los Angeles, my new signature Taylor guitars (DDSM or Doyle Dykes Signature Model) were debuted. Each guitar is adorned with a beautiful white rose inlay in abalone and mother-of-pearl shell on the headstock. The folks at Taylor chose this because they were wanting something special to depict my personality and character without just having a signature of my name. This is the story that inspired that idea.

It was in 1980 that I moved my family from Nashville, Tennessee, back to my hometown of Jacksonville, Florida, and began performing primarily in churches as a ministry. I had previously left the Grandpa Jones show and playing on the Grand Ole Opry as well as playing in the studios as a session guitarist. We bought a small home and were quite happy to be closer to our families. However, I had just begun to pray about our house situation. Our home was on a busy street, and we needed more space for our growing family. It wasn't easy making a living traveling around playing mostly in small churches. I knew it would be a miracle to find a larger home at that time . . . but I still prayed about it.

One night, after performing at a church in Savannah, Georgia, about three hours away, I got home about midnight. Rita met me at the door while holding our youngest daughter, Holli. Heidi, our

oldest daughter, was standing right next to her with a big grin on her face. Rita gave me a kiss and a hug and said, "Good night . . . they're yours!" The girls giggled as I began to chase them around the house, and we played until about 2:30 a.m., which I sometimes explain as "normal musician hours."

She just kept looking at me with those big brown eyes as if she wanted to tell me something.

Since it was already so late, I put them to bed without a bedtime story, and our prayers, too, were shortened. Holli fell asleep even before the Amen, but Heidi was wide awake. I remember telling Heidi how late it was and that she needed to go to sleep, but she just kept looking at me with those big brown eyes as if she wanted to tell me something. After all, I didn't say a normal prayer, and for that I felt bad. I left for a moment then peeked in to see if she was still awake. Of course she was, and I sensed she wanted something.

I went back into her room and knelt by her bed and asked if there was anything special she wanted to ask God for. She said, "Well, there is something that I've been thinking about . . . do you think God would give me a rose if we asked Him?"

"A rose?" I asked. "Why would you like to have a rose?" She said, "Because I think they're so pretty and I've always wanted one! Can we ask God to bring me one?" So I agreed, and we asked God to bring a rose for Heidi. *Anything to get her to go to sleep* was also in my thoughts. Besides, what would it hurt? I also admired her childlike faith that Jesus spoke about in Matthew the eighteenth chapter and how precious it was. I had actually been speaking to some friends of mine about childlike faith and what it really meant. I even spoke about it in my concerts.

I was amused by her simple little request but then thought of my big needs as a father and provider for my family. I was really trying to make ends meet hoping that Rita could stay home with the girls. I was already traveling a lot and it wouldn't have been possible without her being there with the children. I also remembered the larger home we had been praying for. I really needed some childlike faith of my own. Nevertheless, by the next day I had already forgotten Heidi's request.

It was a beautiful day in Jacksonville that day. I remember taking Rita to the hospital to see one of her friends who had just had a baby. Because it was in a section that my daughters couldn't visit, I happily took them down the street to a park and walked them around a 250-year-old oak tree called the "Treaty Oak," which was a very historical tree. Around the tree was a beautiful rose garden in full bloom. It was funny that I never thought about Heidi's rose that day. In fact, Heidi didn't mention it either. The roses were all red and it still didn't click in my mind until later that night at prayer time about Heidi's prayer request.

Later that night after their bedtime story, Heidi grabbed my hand and said, "It's time to say our prayers now!" As we began to pray, I felt her little hand tremble and heard her sobbing as tears were streaming down her little face. I asked her what was wrong and she asked, "How come God didn't bring my rose to me today? Do you think He forgot?"

What kind of answer could I give to her? This was a God question and I was just a young father. How could I explain it to her? I could have said, "In His time," or, "If it be His will!" I didn't say any of those things. Remember, she was only four years old.

Suddenly I thought about the roses in the park that day. I said, "Heidi, remember those beautiful roses we saw in the park today? God made those for you and for Holli and me just so we could enjoy them!" I thought that was pretty clever, even though I didn't think of it while we were actually there in the park. (Duh!)

Then, Heidi asked if they were really ours why I didn't pick one for her. I suddenly remembered a sign that said DON'T PICK THE ROSES: CITY OF JACKSONVILLE and explained that to her. Then she shook her head as if to say no and said, "Daddy—I want one I can hold in my hand. Can't God bring me a rose of my own?" Heidi held out her little chubby hand as if she were holding one already.

I mentioned Hebrews 11:1 in the last chapter: "Now faith is the substance of things hoped for, the evidence of things not seen" (KJV) and in this instance, it came to mind, too. This was the real deal! This was childlike faith. Something sort of went off in my spirit and I took her little hand and said, "You know, we didn't mention the color of the rose!" (I also thought that was a pretty clever answer for me as a father.) She said, "Did He need to know that? I wanted a white one! That's what I've been thinking about!" (That totally blew the whole idea of the rose garden, since they were all in red.)

It was then that I told Heidi about the prayer of agreement and how Jesus said in Matthew 18:19 that "if two of you shall agree on earth as touching anything that they shall ask, it shall be done for them of my Father which is in heaven" (KJV). I also love the Amplified version where it reads, "Again I tell you, if two of you on earth agree (harmonize together, make a symphony together) about whatever [anything and everything] they may ask, it will come to pass and be done for them by My Father in heaven."

Heidi said, "Well, I'm in agreement!" We joined hands once again and "agreed" for a white rose for Heidi. After that, I went to bed and could hardly sleep, thinking about Heidi's white rose and how serious she was about getting one from the Lord. Indeed, it had to come from "Him."

Wouldn't you know, the next morning when I got up, all of these things came to mind, like call the florist down the street or ask a friend to come by and bring a white rose home to Heidi. You see, I had to go out of town again that day for a concert and all these "plan Bs" swarmed into my head like bees to a . . . well, a flower. I didn't do any of those things and decided to stay with "plan A." Besides, Heidi was much too inquisitive and would have asked if I had done it or if it actually came from God. All day I thought of the rose and prayed and asked God to do this for her.

That night, I performed a concert in a church in central Florida for some friends of mine who pastored there. It was a small church building with an aisle right down the center of the sanctuary. After my concert, it didn't take long for the congregation to clear the building. I was putting away my guitars and was about to join the pastor and his wife for some refreshments at their home next door to the church.

Suddenly I heard a voice coming from the back of the building. "Are you Doyle Dykes?" I was putting away my guitars and just set one down on a stand and I told her that I was. She replied, "I was in my garden today and God told me to bring this to you, Brother Dykes!"

I had never been to this church before. I only knew the pastor and his wife because she had recorded an album in Tennessee and I was lead guitarist on it. I had never seen this lady before, but I could tell that she was special. She was perhaps in her thirties, but she was like a child. She was carrying a package in her hand. It was long and slender with a wrapper made of aluminum foil. I replied, "God told you to give me that?" She again said yes and how she had been in her garden and the Lord instructed her to bring this package to me.

I supposed it to be something from a vegetable garden and envisioned a carrot or an onion or something edible. (That must be a guy thing—always thinking of food!) She handed me the package and I replied, "I'll enjoy eating this from your garden, ma'am!" She then said to me, "Well, you'd better not eat that . . . you'd better look at it!" As I gently peeled open the little foil package, I remember seeing this sort of off-white, naturally beautiful rose petal. I stood there in disbelief. I closed the package, then opened it up again. I could hardly believe my tear-filled eyes. It was a single little solitary white rose. Heidi's rose.

I was completely blown away! I mean, here I am, "God's man of faith and power," surprised and taken by this simple gift. To me it was huge! To some people miracles are only about getting big things like a home, a new job, or physical healing. I've often said that if you can't see God in the little things, then perhaps you wouldn't recognize Him in the big ones either.

I've often said that if you can't see God in the little things, then perhaps you wouldn't recognize Him in the big ones either.

I looked at the rose and then at the lady, and then looked at the rose again. Suddenly I felt ashamed because I don't think I would have chosen her. I mean, had I known that this little miracle would come that night by someone in the audience, perhaps I would have looked around and picked someone else, like the pastor or someone who looked a bit more "spiritual" than her. Maybe if I was trying to find someone there to bring a miracle to a little girl, I would have picked someone who looked "normal" to me. In fact, I would have probably dismissed the entire crowd!

I've learned a few things in my life. As I heard an old minister from Wales, "Uncle Arthur Burt," say, "I'm not 'claiming' but I'm 'aiming' to be a better husband, father, Christian". . . and so on. I learned especially through this that God can use anyone He wants to carry out His plan. I've also learned that we shouldn't sum people up so quickly by the way they act or dress. We often look so much at the appearance but still, God looks at the heart.

As I held this little miracle in my hand, all I could say was, "This isn't mine!" The lady looked at me and in a very matter-of-fact tone said "Well, God told me to bring that to you from my garden, Brother Dykes!" I agreed and then told her the story of Heidi's prayer just the night before and how the Lord used her that day to bring the desire of a little girl. She just smiled and nodded and said, "Okay— that's nice!" That was good enough for her. She didn't even act surprised.

THE BEAUTIFUL WHITE ROSE INLAY ON MY GUITAR HAS ALLOWED ME TO SHARE THIS STORY ALL OVER THE WORLD.

I was still slack-jawed and could hardly believe it. You see, she had childlike faith too. If we believe our Heavenly Father who spared not His own Son but will "with Him" freely give us all things—then, we shouldn't be surprised either. (Romans 8:32, paraphrase mine.)

She turned and started walking away down the aisle. I watched every step she made. I really wondered if she were an angel. After all, there was no one left in the building. I thought maybe she'd float away. I found out later her parents were an elderly couple and had brought her to the concert that night, and perhaps she had waited until the end to bring her little gift to me. I learned she had been raised in that very church from a child. But to me, she also certainly did the job of an angel that night!

After I finished packing my guitars, I walked over to the parsonage and needless to say, went in with an emotional high. I shared my story with the pastor and his wife. They also were in tears. They knew the lady and were very fond of her and affirmed to me that she could definitely hear the voice of God. I ended up staying overnight since it had gotten so late. The pastor's wife put the white rose in a vase and before I left for home, she wrapped it back up in the same little foil package just as I received it.

*Doyle's
2002 Taylor
Doyle Dykes
Signature Model
Desert Rose
Limited*

The next day when I pulled up in my driveway, Heidi ran out to meet me. She climbed up and gave me a big hug before I could even get out of the driver's seat in my van. I reached over on the dashboard for the little package and handed it to her. I said, "Here's a present for you, Heidi!" She smiled and said, "He brung it, didn't He, Daddy! I knew God would bring my rose!" She opened the little package and then said, "And it's a white one!" She jumped out of the van and started running toward the house. I can still hear the slamming of our screen door and the sound of her little shrill voice as she was crying, "Mommy . . . Mommy . . . God brung my rose to me today!" That's just how she said it. God "brung" her rose that day for sure.

There is one other thing that I noticed. Heidi wasn't at all surprised! Just like the little lady who had delivered it didn't seem surprised either. Delighted perhaps — but not surprised. I feel this is another golden attribute of childlike faith. Why should we be "childish" in our faith? I think it's so we can see how "Fatherish" God really is!

In 1994 I wrote the song "White Rose for Heidi" and recorded it on my first all-instrumental CD (*Fingerstyle Guitar*). The folks at Taylor guitars heard it and it also helped open the door for my Windham Hill/BMG record deal. In fact, the entire theme of my album on Windham Hill, *Gitarre 2000*, seemed to center around a single white rose. I've told this story all over the world and even shared it on the secular shows I mentioned at the beginning of chapter 2 (the *Mark & Brian Show* in Los Angeles on KLOS radio and the *Steve & Johnnie Show* on WGN in Chicago).

People all over ask me about the rose on my signature Taylor guitar and I tell them. Once I was speaking with Pastor Rick Warren at Saddleback Church in Lake Forest, California. He was admiring my guitar and asked me about the beautiful rose on the headstock. As I was telling him the story, his assistant asked if he'd sign a copy of his book for Michael Jordan who had requested it. They took a photo as he signed it. He apologized for the interruption and asked me to continue with this story. He paused and looked at me with a truthful sincerity in his eyes and said, "That's an incredible story!" I said thanks, I've been asked to put it in a book. It dawned on me that he has the largest selling nonfiction book in history next to the Bible. This was not only a compliment but an affirmation that stories like this can only come from the Lord.

Then there are artists such as Roger Whittaker, Taylor Swift, Carolyn Dawn Johnson, Martin Barre (Jethro Tull), Gregg Allman (the Allman Brothers Band), and Dwayne "the Rock" Johnson, who have all played my signature Taylor guitars with the white rose on the headstock.

MY WIFE RITA, OUR DAUGHTER HEIDI, AND ME AT GRANDPA AND RAMONA JONES' HOME IN GOODLETTSVILLE, TN OUTSIDE NASHVILLE IN 1977. I STILL LOVE THOSE GIRLS!

On October 1, 2004, I walked Heidi down the aisle at her wedding as my brother, Aubrey Dykes, played a song I wrote for Heidi— appropriately called "White Rose for Heidi"—on the piano. Today, she's a nurse anesthetist and resides in Florida with her husband, Tom Dixon, and their son, Andrew, and beautiful little daughter, Leila Grace. Tom spoke with me before he proposed to Heidi and asked what I thought would be an appropriate setting and someplace special to propose to her. I suggested the park next to the Treaty Oak where she and I had looked at the roses all those years ago. There was a big fountain across the street, which is the same place I proposed to her mother. So, as the story goes on with time, it seems to grow even more as if turning into a beautiful bouquet of white roses.

To this day Heidi still loves white roses. And she still gets them. I think it's okay for her mom and me to send roses once in a while. Heidi's husband, Tom, does too. He also loves this story and it has already become a part of their lives together.

And what about the house I was praying for? We got it. In fact, we've had lots of houses since that time. You know, I couldn't even tell you the address on that house I prayed for, but I'll never ever forget the rose. You see, sometimes the little miracles become touchstones in our lives and change us forever.

I'm certainly not an author, but I am delighted to share with you this little true story about childlike faith and the prayer of agreement that continues to be a part of our daily lives. Childlike faith is the only kind of faith that pleases God. "And He called a little child to Himself and put him in the midst of them, and said, Truly I say to you, unless you repent (change, turn about) and become like little children [trusting, lowly, loving, forgiving], you can never enter the kingdom of heaven [at all]. Whoever will humble himself therefore and become like this little child [trusting, lowly, loving, forgiving is greatest in the kingdom of heaven" (Matthew 18:2-4, AMP).

The night the little lady handed me the rose, I saw the lights of faith . . . not just any kind of faith but childlike faith, which is the kind of faith that pleases God. I also saw the lights of love—the love of our Heavenly Father as I held this little solitary white rose in my own hands. Our lives have not been the same since that time. This story is a part of us. It's family stuff. So many times when we are praying for something, we will remember it—and being able to share it with you in this book is yet another . . . White Rose for Heidi.

To watch Doyle play "White Rose for Heidi,"
pop in your DVD or go to
www.doyledykes.com/tlom.htm

FAVORITE SCRIPTURES FOR THIS CHAPTER

Romans 8:32

"He who did not spare His own Son, but delivered Him up
for us all, how shall He not with Him also freely give us all things?"

Matthew 18:3–4

". . . Assuredly, I say to you, unless you are converted
and become as little children, you will by no means
enter the kingdom of heaven. Therefore whoever
humbles himself as this little child is the
greatest in the kingdom of heaven."

Matthew 18:19

"Again I say to you that if two of you agree on earth
concerning anything that they ask,
it will be done for them by My Father in heaven."

Hebrews 11:1

"Now faith is the substance of things hoped for,
the evidence of things not seen."

Matthew 6:28

"So why do you worry about clothing?
Consider the lilies of the field, how they
grow: they neither toil nor spin . . ."

Guitar Tuning for "White Rose for Heidi"

C G D G B D

First recorded on my *Fingerstyle Guitar* CD.

Also recorded on Windham Hill/BMG *Gitarre 2000* CD.

CHAPTER 9

The Visitation

I have always tried to be involved in my children's plans and dreams for their future. What's wonderful about that is that they seem to want me to be. At the same time, I've always tried to include them in what I do as well. My daughter Heidi has sung with me on the streets of remote towns and auditoriums in Brazil and across America. My daughters Holli and Haley have appeared with me also across America and Europe and have even performed numerous times on the Grand Ole Opry.

My son Caleb has also recorded with me and played in many venues where I would feature him on guitar. I really try not to overpromote my own children, but to me this is sharing the joy of my life. I'm proud of them, and I so want them to include me in their lives. As long as they were living at home or still under my "covering" as a father, I truly believed God to guide and direct them, and He always has. This is not only my responsibility but my privilege and desire. However, they sometimes still have different ideas of how they want to do things.

Our oldest daughter, Heidi, was in college in Cleveland, Tennessee, and making excellent grades, but she wanted to move to Nashville and go to Belmont University to enroll in their nursing program. I had actually moved my family to Cleveland from Nashville in order to have them enroll at Lee University and stay close to home—and now here's Heidi wanting to move back to Nashville and go to nursing school. The only thing was, it was also very expensive and I really didn't have the funds to send her. On top of that, our daughter Holli was also about to begin classes at Lee University. Help me Jesus!

It was March 29, 1996, and I was staying at a Holiday Inn near Dallas off Interstate 20. I was going to play at a men's fellowship breakfast the next morning, and here I was feeling like the worst father of all because for the first time my daughters really needed me, and I couldn't provide for them. I remember so vividly thinking of my brother-in-law Buddy Tyrrell and how he saved for his two sons' college since they were infants. As I've mentioned, during those years I was a pastor at a small church in Jacksonville, Florida, and sold everything when I went back to playing my guitar again. I'm not complaining, and

For the first time my daughters really needed me, and I couldn't provide for them.

it was my choice, but I needed some help. I took out the Gideon Bible from the nightstand in my hotel room and began reading Scriptures such as Philippians 4:19 (KJV): "My God shall supply all your need according to his riches in glory by Christ Jesus." After reading the Word I turned out the lights and opened the curtain and just talked to the Lord like this: "Lord, this is Your Word, this is what YOU said You'd do and I really need for You to go to bat for me this time!"

I wasn't just praying for my daughters, I was praying for money! Sometimes we just have to have a blessing from the Father. I had nowhere else to turn. I felt I needed to just play my guitar in a state of thanksgiving and just play to Him!

I took my guitar out of the case and began to minister to the Lord and play whatever was in my head — or spirit, if you please. I remember playing this melody that seemed familiar, yet I know I had never played it before. I stood up to my feet and began to play the chorus or bridge, and that's when I began to play things I'd never played before or even seen anyone else play before. I began to weep as I played because I felt His presence in a very special way. I felt a confidence and encouragement that made me feel as though my Father was there with me and I was just enjoying being a son. The heaviness and guilt was gone. I didn't have the answer yet, but I definitely had the solution. This is when it's easy to cast "all your care upon Him, for He cares for you" because you feel He's right there in the same room (1 Peter 5:7). Believe me, it's not scary but totally wonderful! Where His Presence is, there is Peace.

Doyle's 1995 Taylor Custom Presentation Brazilian

I also knew I had a special visit from the Lord because of the things I was doing on the guitar. It was like, "Man, I wish I'd thought of that first!" When I got home I made up an intro and ended up taking it into the studio and recorded it on my *HEAT* album. I also later included it on my Windham Hill/ BMG recording *Gitarre 2000*. Many people feel it's the best song I've ever written. Personally I feel I only played it that night for the first time and just never forgot it! I still feel I had little to do with writing it.

A few days later I was playing at the Grand Ole Opry on Saturday night, and the next afternoon I was on the Opry stage for another special occasion. It was Grandpa and Ramona Jones's fiftieth wedding anniversary, and they had invited me to come and play. Of course all the stars from the Opry showed up and the other guest invited to play was the legendary Mr. John Hartford, whom I'd admired since I was a child.

I'll never forget standing there playing as the Grand Ole Opry manager Bob Whittaker took Chet over to watch me play. Chet asked if I'd come over and play a guest spot with him at the Cafe Milano the next night. I was also taping a television show on TNN that same day called *Prime Time Country*. Normally I would've been more excited to be on that television show but the chance

THE GUITAR ALWAYS SEEMS TO BE AHEAD OF ME AS A PLAYER. I'M ALWAYS LEARNING NEW THINGS FROM IT!

to be onstage with Chet once again was such a huge thing for me. This was Chet's version of what Les Paul had done in New York City for so many years at the Iridium Club.

After doing the sound check, I walked into Chet's dressing room and just hung out for awhile. It was a memorable occasion for me. Janis Ian was also on the show that night. Chet appreciated all types and styles of music especially if they were creative and had their own thing going. Chet was arguably the most influential guitar player on the planet and my number one guitar hero! I brought my guitar to his dressing room and played "The Visitation" for him. Chet loved instrumental songs with a nice melody and I thought he'd like it,

Doyle's custom thumbpick made by Fred Kelly.

but the main reason I did it was to see if I had heard him play this particular thing I was doing or if it really was Divinely Inspired.

As I played, Chet just watched and said, "Well, you have your bass going and then arpeggio harmonics and a tremolo at the same time." I asked, "Chet, have you ever done that?" He said, "I've never seen anyone do that before! Where'd you learn that?" I explained how I wrote it as I was praying for my kids and it just came. "So I guess the Holy Spirit knows how to play the guitar!" Chet said, "I'll say He does!" That was all I needed!

Sometimes when times seem to be grim and you don't know what to do, that's when you minister to the Lord and give thanks. I've heard it said that there are two times to Praise the Lord . . . when you feel like it and when you don't! I'm also convinced that there are two times to thank the Lord—of course, after you get what you're praying for, but perhaps even more importantly, give thanks before you ever see it!

I feel if we'll spend more time "thanking" than just "thinking," we'll see more results and answers to our prayers.

As you'll see later on, we got our answer, but it was after we acted in faith and enrolled Heidi at Belmont. Our answer was soon on the way, but in my "knower" I knew God would help us in our situation. In the meantime, I had a new song and some things on the guitar that have become part of my signature style. I feel if we'll spend more time "thanking" than just "thinking," we'll see more results and answers to our prayers. I'm so delighted that even when things aren't looking so good His presence is still near! All I know is, in Dallas, Texas, at a Holiday Inn, I had a visit from the Lord. Once again, God shined His light upon my situation. The lights of Comfort, Encouragement, Divine Inspiration, and Creativity came into my hotel room that night! I'm so thankful to know Him and experience Him in such a way!

1994
My first
Taylor 20th
Anniversary
Rosewood

To watch Doyle play "The Visitation," pop in your DVD or go to
www.doyledykes.com/tlom.htm

Favorite Scriptures for This Chapter

Philippians 4:13
"I have strength for all things in Christ Who empowers me
[I am ready for anything and equal to anything
through Him Who infuses inner strength into me;
I am self-sufficient in Christ's sufficiency]." (AMP)

John 16:23
"And in that day you will ask Me nothing.
Most assuredly, I say to you, whatever you ask
the Father in My name He will give you."

Mark 11:22–24
"So Jesus answered and said to them, 'Have faith in God.
For assuredly, I say to you, whoever says to this mountain,
"Be removed and be cast into the sea," and does not doubt
in his heart, but believes that those things he says will be done,
he will have whatever he says. Therefore I say to you,
whatever things you ask when you pray, believe that you
receive them, and you will have them.'"

Proverbs 8:12
"I, wisdom, dwell with prudence,
and find out knowledge and discretion."

Tuning for "The Visitation"
CGDGBE

*Doyle's 1995 Taylor Custom
Presentation Brazilian*

CHAPTER 10

Who Gets the Spotlight?

October 4, 1997, was a special night for me at the Grand Ole Opry. I had already been appearing on the Opry for over a year as a soloist, and things were going well for me. I had just been featured in a major guitar magazine, so there was a sort of buzz among the musicians at the Opry that night. I didn't realize that until I was approached by Jeff Hannah and some of the boys from the Nitty Gritty Dirt Band, who said they were anxious to hear me play. I wasn't used to this type of attention since (as I mentioned earlier) most of my life I'd been "Internationally Unknown"! A lot of my favorite musicians and singers were on the show that night as well, such as Vince Gill, who of course is also a fine picker. I knew I had to do well and prove myself to all these guys.

Well, at least that's what I thought I knew.

We had been visiting around with some of our good friends that night at the Opry. Rita and our kids were all there, so it was really a special night for me. Earlier that day at home, I had to change strings in a rush on my new prototype Taylor guitar with this unique pickup system by L. R. Baggs called the hexaphonic system, which meant each string had its own little pickup. So I threw it in the van and we all headed for the Opry.

I would always get nervous playing the Opry, and this night, as I said, was just a little more special for me having all this added attention. It's funny, but even now I get a "charley horse" in my middle toe on my right foot when I'm on the Opry stage. I can play other venues with several times the size of the crowd, but I suppose the Opry is such a special place to me personally it has

GUITARS DON'T MAKE ME NERVOUS, PEOPLE DO!

that effect on me. So if you see me stomping around onstage a lot at the Ryman or the Grand Ole Opry House, it's because the middle toe on my right foot is KILLING ME!

I remember my daughters Holli and Haley coming to me as I was talking to a stagehand who told me that I was about to go on. I said, "Okay, girls . . . I have no time to warm up so let's just say a prayer and I'll grab my guitar and get out there!" We joined hands and I prayed, "Lord, we just ask You to do something we haven't even thought of tonight. Go beyond us! We ask You to Fill the House with Your Presence tonight! As I minister to You tonight with my guitar, I ask You to minister to Your people!" It wasn't long before I totally forgot about that prayer.

I didn't even look at my guitar and check it out before I went on, as I had been in such a hurry that day. We live about two and a half hours from the Opry so it was a bit of a drive getting there. When they introduced me that night, I walked out and said, "When I play a song like this, I'm really playing to Him" (as I pointed my index finger upward). "I found out that if I minister to Him, He'll minister to His people!"

I thought, "Oh no, what's wrong with my new guitar!"

I paused and looked at each section of the audience that night and said, "I don't have the power to blow the fuzz off of a Georgia peach, but I know someone who does, and He can give you what you need tonight." I know that may be a little preachy (or peachy) for the Grand Ole Opry, but this song was not about me. I was about to play "How Great Thou Art."

When I first began playing the song, everything seemed normal to me, but when I got to the first chorus and started to play a little more aggressively, everything seemed to be falling apart. I thought, *Oh no, what's wrong with my new guitar!* Some of the strings seemed to be louder than the others and they weren't spaced evenly. I started getting really nervous. To me it sounded, as Grandpa Jones would have said, "like a two-by-four strung up with baling wire!" And the worst thing, it was me!

I was so shook up I didn't even remember whether or not I played the second chorus. All I knew was I just wanted to get off that stage! I was so embarrassed. I was so into trying to impress everyone with my professionalism I had completely forgotten what I had just said to the audience about ministering to Him. As I was trying to gather up my thirty-foot guitar cable (which seemed like 300 feet), I remember the host of the show (and my good friend and brother) Billy Walker coming out and giving me a big hug and squeezing my face up to his rhinestone studded suit. I think I had a butterfly pattern imprinted on my face from his jacket for a week. He hollered out, "Have you ever heard anything like that?" I wanted to say, "No Billy, and I really hate that IT WAS ME!!!"

Doyle's 2000 Taylor Doyle Dykes Signature Model Prototype

I felt like ole Billy just felt sorry for me. Then, as I was almost off the stage, Bob Whittaker, the Opry manager, took me by the arm and led me back to center stage and grabbed a microphone and said, "Put the spotlight back over here and let's hear it again for Doyle Dykes!" I just knew by then they were all feeling sorry for me! I thought as I was playing, *They'll never have me here again.* Then, after all this I just wanted to cry, thinking of how nice they were to come out and rescue me like that.

As I finally made it off the stage, another Opry star, Jeannie Seely, grabbed my arm and with tears in her eyes said, "Doyle, I was on my way here from the Cracker Barrel and heard you. I just feel something when you play a song like that!" I thought how nice she was to also help pick me up after such a terrible performance. I almost ran to the dressing room after that and packed up my guitar and headed for the van. I remember Rita talking with our good friends the Whites, and I told her that the kids and I would see her outside in the van.

I threw my guitar in the back and sat in the driver's seat, having the biggest Pity Party anyone could ever throw for themselves. My daughters Holli and Haley got in the van first and both were raving about what had just happened. "Wow Dad, that's the best you've ever done," Haley said. Holli chimed in too with "Yeah Dad, that was awesome!"

By this time I'd had enough. I said, "Okay, girls, you know good and well that is the worst thing that's ever happened to me! I don't know what went wrong but I think something was wrong with my new guitar. I don't think I can ever come back here again!" (I looked at it later and sure enough, I hadn't installed the strings properly because some of the strings were sitting on the little saddles and some were just stuck in between, which totally threw the performance of the system for a loop! In other words, it was my fault.)

Holli replied, "Dad, you saw what Billy Walker did and we've never seen Bob Whittaker run out onstage like that for anybody!"

"Well, I guess they were just being nice because they felt sorry for me," I said.

It was then that Haley said, "Dad, He did what we asked Him to do . . . He Filled the House with His Presence!"

That's when it hit me like a ton of bricks. I was so completely engulfed in my own self-motivation and shameless self-promotion (which quickly, I might add, turned to self-pity), I missed the whole event! *None of this was about me!* God showed up and people

"None of this was about me!" God showed up and people responded.

responded. I am convinced this is really what the anointing of the Holy Spirit is—God showing Himself!

I didn't sleep very well that night. We were up early the next morning in order to get to a church for a concert. It was cold, and everyone else had just curled up and gone back to sleep. I was wide awake! It was like I couldn't wait for an explanation. I needed an answer and I felt it was coming . . . and it did!

I'll never forget what I said. "Lord, nothing like this has ever happened to me before and especially on one of my favorite places to play, the Grand Ole Opry. If You're trying to tell me something, I'm listening!" Please understand that I don't use the phrase very often that "God spoke to me," but that morning, without a doubt—He did!

Again, I played "How Great Thou Art." He said, "Son . . . My Greatness . . . Does Not Depend . . . on YOURS!"

It was so real to me! I pondered for a moment because it was so simple, yet so profound. I actually said out loud, "Okay, Lord, I want You to know I got it the first time . . . please don't let anything like that happen again!" And it hasn't. Thank You Jesus!!!!

As I'm finishing writing this chapter, I'm actually sitting in the green room at Saddleback Church and listening to Pastor Rick Warren speaking on reaching the world with the gospel. At this very moment he is making the official announcement that Saddleback missionaries have now preached the Gospel of Jesus Christ to every nation in the world, thereby doing their part toward fulfilling the Great Commission. Of course Pastor Rick's leadership and his fantastic team are much to be credited. But Pastor Rick gives all the credit to the everyday people in the church who've given their hard-earned finances as well as their time in volunteering and actually carrying this message themselves right from this local congregation. They tell me most of this accomplishment comes from the small group ministries who want to do something significant for God. Although nothing we could ever do in this life could compare with the Greatness of God, it is evident that God's greatness can certainly be seen in and through us.

In fact, that's the way God chooses to work most of the time — ordinary people doing extraordinary things for the kingdom of God. It takes getting out of our comfort zones sometimes. In a few moments, I'll finish the service by playing "How Great Thou Art."

That night at the Opry I saw the lights on the stage of the Grand Ole Opry. I felt the bright spotlight shine on my face when Bob Whittaker said, "Turn the spotlight back over here," but I didn't really see it. I didn't want to hear it anymore for myself.

I knew something had gone wrong and I didn't really see any lights or hear the audience. I think I was the only one who knew that night that something was wrong. Perhaps I

I KNOW WHAT I CAN DO WITH A GUITAR IN MY HANDS . . . .
BUT NOTHING (OR NO ONE) CAN BE COMPARED TO
THE FEELING YOU GET WHEN GOD FILLS THE HOUSE!

was even the only one who thought it was really that terrible. The Holy Spirit indeed showed up that night at the Grand Ole Opry. He showed up especially for me. I know that Jesus referred to the Holy Spirit as "the Comforter." But honestly, that night He wasn't very comfortable. God corrects those He loves as a father corrects his children. Early that morning on October 5, 1997, I saw the lights of God's love—the love of my Father in heaven. I also saw the lights of Greatness. His Greatness . . . regardless of mine.

HOW GREAT THOU ART IS A SONG THAT IS BIGGER THAN THE GUITAR OR THE PLAYER. SOMETIMES WHEN I PLAY THAT SONG IT FEELS EFFORTLESS, YET IT'S THE MOST POWERFUL SONG I'VE EVER PLAYED.

You won't find "How Great Thou Art" on your DVD
but if you'd like to watch Doyle play it, go to
www.doyledykes.com/tlom.htm

FAVORITE SCRIPTURES FOR THIS CHAPTER

Psalm 33:3

"Sing to Him a new song;
play skillfully with a shout of joy."

Psalm 145:3

"Great is the LORD, and greatly to be praised;
and His greatness is unsearchable."

Proverbs 3:12

"For whom the LORD loves He corrects,
just as a father the son in whom he delights."

Hebrews 12:5–6

"And you have forgotten the exhortation
which speaks to you as to sons: 'My son, do not despise
the chastening of the LORD, nor be discouraged
when you are rebuked by Him; for whom
the LORD loves He chastens,
and scourges every son whom He receives.'"

*1994–My first Taylor
20th Anniversary
Rosewood*

CHAPTER II

Meeting Mr. Stringfield

A few weeks had gone by since I had experienced "The Visitation" that night in the hotel room in Dallas. I was playing on the Grand Ole Opry on a Friday night. I remember walking toward the stage and looked over at my daughter Haley, who was walking next to me holding my guitar cable so it wouldn't drag on the floor. Suddenly I felt that I should ask her to sing "Amazing Grace." She was about fourteen years old then and wasn't necessarily dressed up to sing in front of several thousand people that night. I said, "Haley, I'd like for you to sing 'Amazing Grace' tonight—is that okay?"

Now lots of people would've said, I'm not dressed for this or we haven't practiced or something. She just smiled at me and said, "O thank you, Daddy!" I thought to myself, *That little monkey. She's not scared or nervous at all!* I had played a tune with the band and then looked back at Haley, and as she walked up toward the microphone, I whispered to her, "Sing to Him," and she did! That night I felt the presence of God once again. Someone once told me that they thought what we call the "anointing" is simply God showing up! Whether in a church or at the Grand Ole Opry or wherever, people respond when they sense God's presence, and that night was no exception.

Whether in a church or at the Grand Ole Opry or wherever, people respond when they sense God's presence.

As we walked off the stage this man approached me in a red Western shirt, cowboy hat, blue jeans, boots, and a belt buckle about as wide as he was. He held his hand out for a handshake and said, "I don't know why I don't know you, but I believe God wants me to be your friend!" He went on to tell me how he lived across the street from Chet Atkins and said he was sure Chet had probably mentioned me to him but he'd never heard or seen me before. I told him we were to play the next day at the Chet Atkins Appreciation Society Convention in Nashville and he said he had already planned on being there.

The next day Mr. Stringfield told me some stories about Chet I thought interesting. Mr. Stringfield was a strong believer and said he and Chet would take walks together in the mornings and have conversations about Christ. He also assured me that Chet Atkins was a believer and had been for a long time although he was rather shy about expressing it in the way some people do. Mr. Stringfield shared how much he enjoyed what we did at the Opry the night before. He asked me about my entire family and I had already introduced him to Haley and Holli who were there and told him about my wife, Rita, and our son, Caleb, and our other daughter, Heidi, who was visiting relatives in Florida that weekend. He assured me that he'd be praying for my family. What a nice and interesting man Mr. Stringfield was.

A few days passed and I was outside doing yard work at our home. Rita called out to me and said that a Mr. Stringfield was on the phone. I ran into the house and he said, "Doyle, I've been praying for you and your family this week and I have all the names of your children except for the daughter who wasn't with you last weekend. What is her name again?" I told him about Heidi and he went on to say how he didn't know exactly why but really felt he should be praying for me and my family. He told me that he wanted to meet Heidi someday too and I told him that she had gone up to Nashville that day to look for a job.

Doyle's 1962 Gretsch Chet Atkins 6120 (a gift from boyhood barber, Harvey Simmons)

"Really, well, what kind of job is she looking for?" he asked.

I told him she applied at the mall and a child care facility. She was looking for any available job that would help with her college expenses. As I mentioned in chapter 9, she was transferring to Belmont University, which meant more money for dorm and food expenses. We had already enrolled her and I was still praying for a miracle because I still didn't know how we were going to pay for it. (Remember too that Heidi's sister Holli was also beginning her first semester at Lee University in Cleveland, Tennessee.)

Mr. Stringfield asked me where Heidi planned to go to college and what she was majoring in. When I told him she was going to Belmont University for nursing school, he exclaimed, "Well, I work at Baptist Hospital in Nashville so please have her come by and see me. I may be able to introduce her to some of the nurses here. If she's still in town, please tell her to go to the hospital and ask for David Stringfield. They all know me around here, I've been here for so long." I had no idea if he was in maintenance or some kind of receptionist or guard, or what he did there. I actually had him pictured as a volunteer or a greeter or someone at the information booth because he had such a warm, gentle spirit about him.

HEIDI AND MY DOYLE DYKES SIGNATURE MODEL GUITAR PROTOTYPE IN THE HAGUE, HOLLAND. (1999)

But Heidi had called and I gave her the message. She said she'd drop by the hospital that afternoon, mainly just because I asked her to. She was supposed to spend the night in Nashville and come back home the next afternoon, unless she needed to stay over for another interview. Things were getting pretty close time-wise. It was already the middle of July and classes were starting in a month.

I remember being aroused out of deep sleep about four the next morning. "Daddy, Daddy, wake up!" It startled me because at that hour I was afraid something was wrong. We lived about two and a half hours from Nashville and I said, "Heidi, you had to drive half the night to get here!"

"I did!" she said. "I got a job!" "Great, what kind of job?" I asked. "I'm going to be a nurse! They hired me at the hospital!"

By this time I was wide awake. "Daddy, I met your friend Mr. Stringfield. You were right, everybody there knows him! They have a whole WING of the hospital named after him!"

"What? What does he do there?"

She said, "He's the president of the hospital and he introduced me to several directors of nursing and one of them hired me!"

I said, "But Heidi, you haven't even started nursing school yet." She said, "I know, Dad, isn't that cool!" I told her I thought it was kind of scary. "Heidi, I thought they didn't do that sort of thing anymore. That's what they told us at the school."

"They don't," she said. "But they're making an exception!" (They hired Heidi to work within an outpatient surgery setting in the afternoons after her classes.)Then she started crying and said, "But Dad, here's the best part. They're paying for my college! Over fifty thousand dollars! All I have to do is work there after I graduate, which means I'll have a job then too!"

She told me how Mr. Stringfield had displayed in his office letters and tokens of appreciation from athletes and entertainers that he'd helped through the years. Soon after this conversation, he helped Chet Atkins and Grand Ole Opry stars Grandpa Jones, Johnny Russell, and many more. In fact, later on Heidi was actually Johnny Russell's nurse. She called me when I was in Canada and put me on the phone with Johnny. I had been on his portion of the show at the Grand Ole Opry many times. He loved when I played "How Great Thou Art."

Lessons about God's faithfulness weren't the only thing Mr. Stringfield taught me. He told me he called Chet Atkins late one night and woke him up. He said, "I want you to record a song I wrote for my mother!" Chet jokingly said something like, "Well, you know I don't think you can afford that!"

Mr. Stringfield said, "Chet, I'm not kidding. She's dying and I wrote this song for her and I want you to play on it and record it with me so she can hear it—and we need to do it right now!" Chet invited him in and recorded the song. His mother heard it and loved it, and a very short time later she passed away. He said to me, "If you're going to ask someone to do something for you, you may as well ask the very best!" I've lived my life with that attitude ever since.

*Doyle's
2009 Taylor T3*

It's funny, but it seemed I was one of the few people in town who didn't know this man who normally dressed like a Philadelphia lawyer—but that night in July at just the right time, he was this cowboy-looking dude in a red shirt, hat, jeans, boots, and a belt buckle as wide as he was. To me he was a light in a seemingly hopeless situation. The lights of blessing, provision, and promise came just in time through our new friend . . . Mr. Stringfield.

FAVORITE SCRIPTURES FOR THIS CHAPTER

Philippians 4:13
"I can do all things through
Christ who strengthens me."

Psalm 37:25
"I have been young, and now am old;
yet I have not seen the righteous forsaken,
nor his descendants begging bread."

John 15:16
"You did not choose Me,
but I chose you and appointed you
that you should go and bear fruit,
and that your fruit should remain,
that whatever you ask
the Father in My name
He may give you."

*1994–My first Taylor
20th Anniversary Rosewood*

CHAPTER 12

Encounter on a Plane

I think I've made it pretty clear about my feelings being involved with my kids and their futures. I learned about the prayer of agreement when my kids were very small and I've always believed and agreed with them in prayer about things that concerned them and they have for me as well.

One such time was when I had just boarded a plane from Atlanta to Los Angeles and Heidi called me on my cell phone and told me that she felt that she was to move to Florida, which was about eight hours away. (Now believe me, I have no problem with Florida itself, seeing that I was born there. In fact, I'm a third-generation Floridian and my son Caleb and daughter Haley are fourth.) Heidi had mentioned earlier that she had seen an opening with a certain medical group in Tallahassee and was thinking of inquiring. The next thing I knew, she had gone down there on her own and interviewed with them. This is what she was calling me about.

As I mentioned in the last chapter, Heidi worked for Baptist Hospital after she finished nursing school and was encouraged by some of the staff to consider anesthesia as a career. She would be called a "Nurse Anesthetist." I couldn't even pronounce the word "anesthetist" for six months, but we agreed together that God would give us the open door. She was close to the deadline for school acceptance and had already applied for the proper loans and was completing applications.

Wouldn't you know that at just the right time an anesthesiologist walked up to me at the Summer NAMM show in Nashville and offered to make some calls to the school Heidi was interested in on her behalf. Once again I was right "in the way" . . . God's way. The Lord seemed to do this for me just to keep me involved. The interesting thing was, Heidi had such a drive to do things on her own and make her own way, yet when she really needed something, I got involved. Funny thing was, I didn't have a clue. God blesses us behind our backs more than we realize. Besides, He's "Abba" or God our Father or more affectionately, Daddy or Papa—and we dads have to stick together!

She was accepted in the anesthesia program with school tuition paid for in full by a local anesthesia group, who also guaranteed her a job at graduation. I remember Heidi saying to me, "Daddy, every time I need a miracle God always uses you to help me! It's never failed. I'm so glad you're my dad!"

Now how do you think that made me feel? Wow. We both knew it was all God, but it was still so cool how the Lord always put her daddy in the mix of things. It was a tough program, but Heidi graduated with top honors.

The day Heidi called me on the plane about the Florida opportunity, once again she had a deadline and she had to make a decision on where she would work and live. I've noticed in most TV reality shows they're normally fighting some kind of deadline like building a chopper or tricking up somebody's ride or remodeling a house. They always seem stressed to get it done in so many hours or something. There's always pressure because of time, and I've noticed the more pressure . . . the more problems! This can be reality, I suppose, but sometimes we need to "be still and know that HE is God!"

The word "deadline" actually originated from military prisons in the 1800s. They would draw a line in the prison and anyone caught crossing the line would be shot. So do you like "deadlines" now?

I have a friend named Neal Ferry who is a great businessman and my partner in several projects I'm involved with, such as my television show. He told me just recently how decisions made quickly will often work but normally end up being more costly or expensive. He should know, since he's directed multibillion-dollar businesses and is a master decision maker. He's also a believer and knows that decisions "bathed in prayer" are the best!

Doyle's 1958 Fender Telecaster Parts Guitar (a gift from Skip Frye and Kelly Barber)

And now, to continue my story of me being on that plane. I had been very busy and was flying to California for several dates when I found that everything had cancelled except for a concert at a church way up on the top of Big Bear Mountain a couple of hours outside of Los Angeles. I had already booked a flight into a closer airport but changed my flight to Los Angeles in order to be on a larger plane and have a more comfortable seat. The flights were completely full but I managed to get a window seat on a Boeing 767. I had just sat down beside this fellow who looked rather tired, and immediately my cell phone rang. It was Heidi telling me about moving to Tallahassee, Florida. She said, "Daddy, if you had only met these people, you'd know what I mean. Several anesthesiologists including the president of the group, Dr. Henry, and their wives took me to dinner. I was treated with as much respect as if I were interviewing for an MD position. The other nurse anesthetists I met were all so nice. I really feel like I would fit in well with this anesthesia group."

The whole time I was thinking how it seemed so quick and I had not prayed about it. I felt it was a "deadline"!

The flight attendant gave the cell-phone notice so I had to hang up quickly. I told Heidi that I would certainly be praying about it even though I wasn't at all convinced that this was a "God thing."

SOMETIMES WE NEED TO 'BE STILL AND KNOW' THAT HE IS GOD'

Suddenly I dropped my phone as the plane was taxiing down the runway. The man next to me saw me struggling and got up out of his seat to grab my phone for me. I apologized and told him that I wasn't normally all that "busy" and would try and be still for the rest of the flight. I asked if he was from Atlanta, since that was where we were flying out of. He said, "No, I'm from Tallahassee, Florida." He was dressed very casually and appeared to be pretty tired. I said, "Really!" I didn't say anything else to him the rest of the flight because he slept the entire time, which was about four hours. I read letters from our fan base the entire way out and couldn't wait for this guy to wake up so I could ask him some questions about Tallahassee.

When we finally landed in Los Angeles, he woke up and after thinking of all these questions I wanted to ask him, all I could think of was, "So Tallahassee is really growing, I've heard. I just went through there a few weeks ago. It sure is a pretty town with all the oak trees and such."

"Yes," he said, "it's a beautiful town and a great place to live and it really is growing." I said that's interesting because I have a daughter who's thinking of moving there.

"Really, what does your daughter do?" he asked.

"She's a nurse."

"What type of nurse?" he asked. I figured he'd never heard of it but I told him a nurse anesthetist. I was proud that I could finally pronounce it.

Then he told me something that blew my mind. "Well, I'm an anesthesiologist! There are only a couple of anesthesia groups in Tallahassee and I'm the president of one of them. I don't recall interviewing anyone in the last week or so . . . except for one young lady from Tennessee about two weeks ago. Is your daughter named Heidi?"

I felt a jolt of chill bumps all over me in a nanosecond. "Yes!" He put out his hand and said, "I'm (and at the same time we both said) " . . . Dr. Henry!"

I said, "I know who you are! You're the very person Heidi was telling me about on the phone right before we took off in Atlanta, and that's when I dropped my phone."

"You're kidding," he said. We both looked around the plane and he said, "This flight is full and we're sitting next to each other? What are the chances of this happening?" I said, "Pretty good, I think!"

He said, "Well, we were very impressed with your daughter, Mr. Dykes. In fact, more than anyone we've seen in a long time." I said to him, "Let me tell you about my daughter!" For the next four or five minutes as the plane was headed toward the gate, I told him how Heidi had always wanted to be a nurse ever since she was a little girl, and how she graduated at the top of her class. I told him how at times she would put her hand on the patient's head and pray for them. I said she felt it was her calling . . . her ministry if you please! "Well, this is quite amazing," he said. He told me how he had been in surgery early that morning (which explained why he slept so long) and he wasn't able to get away that week when he wanted. His wife and daughters had left a day or so before he did and were meeting him at the baggage claim in the airport. When we got there, he

LES PAUL AND ME IN THE 'GREEN ROOM' AT THE
IRIDIUM CLUB IN NEW YORK CITY. (2002)
WHAT A WONDERFUL MAN AND SUCH A LEGEND
IN OUR WORLD, EVEN TODAY.

introduced me to his wife and daughters. His wife could hardly believe our story.

A few days later Heidi called me as I was about to fly out of New York City after going to see Les Paul at the Iridium Club the night before. I was so excited to tell her about Les Paul and how he asked me to get up and play with him once again, but she was also very excited to tell me the news about Tallahassee.

I'll never forget Heidi describing what happened the days after my meeting Dr. Henry. She told me they had a "roundtable" discussion about hiring her at the anesthesia group. Dr. Henry got up at the meeting and said, "If I've ever felt we needed to hire anybody, it's that girl from Tennessee." He told the story of how we met on the plane and the other doctors were so moved they all agreed unanimously to hire her. In fact, her sign-on bonus was renegotiated in order to include not only her moving expenses, but to pay in full a tuition reimbursement contract she had with a hospital in the Nashville area. Heidi didn't need another dime. Her needs were completely met. She was even able to buy herself her dream car and put a down payment on a new home without a cosigner. She also made a perfect score on her anesthesia board exam for the state of Florida. This was a "God thing" indeed and we were so proud of her and for her success.

The best thing to me about this story is that once again I was in the mix of things in my daughter's life.

The best thing to me about this story is that once again I was in the mix of things in my daughter's life. Now, here is the icing on the cake. Shortly after Heidi moved into her new home, she asked me to be in agreement for God to give her a companion and someone to share her new life with. Two days later, she met the man she was to marry. Mr. Tom Dixon was originally from Pittsburgh, Pennsylvania, but now lived in the very town that I was born in—Jacksonville. Tom's employer had a contract with a hospital in Tallahassee. He had been commuting between the two cities for nearly a year and was looking forward to his last week of this assignment. He met Heidi while in an operating room during those last few days, and the boy was smitten!

It's funny, but he was so much like me the night of that first date I had with Rita. I knew she was the one I was going to marry, and Tom had that same feeling. He continued his "weekly commute" until they were married. It's also funny that (as I mentioned in chapter 8) Tom proposed to Heidi very close to where I proposed to Rita and just down the street from the rose garden where Heidi, Holli, and I were strolling around just before Heidi got her white rose.

Heidi's move to Jacksonville with her new husband couldn't have been planned out any better. It's amazing how God brings things together, even though you've prayed for your kids and their future spouses all their lives! This is truly the work of the "Heavenly Father," who goes far beyond what we earthly fathers can do.

After all that, I've not been as much involved in her personal affairs or her family business—except that today I'm the best grandpa that my perfect little grandkids, Drew and Leila Grace, could ever have! (At least that's what I think!) Tom Dixon's dad is great too but he can write his own book—HA! Oh sure, I'm back in the mix again and maybe, just maybe, it's even a little more fun . . . I do love being a grandpa!

More than ever I'm convinced that there is no such thing as coincidence. I saw the lights of confirmation and extreme direction on a Delta 767 jet and there was nothing scary about it! It was nice of the Lord to keep me in the mix, as well as . . . meeting Dr. Henry.

Favorite Scriptures for This Chapter

Matthew 18:19

"Again I say to you that if two of you
agree on earth concerning anything that they ask,
it will be done for them by My Father in heaven."

Proverbs 16:1

"The preparations of the heart belong to man,
but the answer of the tongue is from the LORD."

Proverbs 16:3

"Commit your works to the LORD,
and your thoughts will be established."

Proverbs 16:9

"A man's heart plans his way,
but the LORD directs his steps."

Psalm 37:31

"The law of his God is in his heart;
none of his steps shall slide."

Psalm 46:10

"Be still, and know that I am God;
I will be exalted among the nations,
I will be exalted in the earth!"

Doyle's 2002 Taylor
Doyle Dykes Signature Model
Desert Rose Limited

CHAPTER 13

The Old Blue-Eyed Preacher (Lights of Warning and Confirmation)

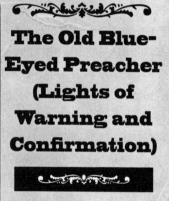

I grew up in the Church of God, and over the years made a lot of friends who became national leaders of that denomination. One such friend was Paul Henson. Brother Paul was the national youth director for the Church of God when I was a teenager and won the teen talent competition for the state of Florida for our denomination. He was also a guitar player and a fine singer and preacher. I've done a lot of meetings with him on a state and local level and, as mentioned in "A Word from an Outlaw," went with him to Trinidad and Tobago in the West Indies.

There were times I felt like quitting, but Brother Paul and his wife, Jeri, were always encouraging me to use my gift of music. They had two sons, Paul Jr. and Tim. Both were in the music business. So music was a big part of this family and when I say they appreciated me . . . they did, and I appreciated and respected them as well.

Brother Paul had become the National Retired Ministers Director for the Church of God. The week before Memorial Day, 2002, he invited me to play at their national convention in my current hometown of Cleveland, Tennessee. I remember playing some fast tunes and then "The Patriotic Medley" and "How Great Thou Art." I was so flattered at the response I got from these ministers who had dedicated their lives to the Gospel of Jesus Christ.

After the program I was up on the stage shaking hands with these ministers, many of whom I'd met through the years and also some I'd never seen before. One such man was an elderly gentleman with the most beautiful blue eyes (besides Grandpa Jones) I think I'd ever seen. He had such a sweet spirit about him. I remember he started the conversation with, "Son, I really enjoyed what you did here tonight but I didn't come up here to flatter you. God sent me to warn you that Satan doesn't like what you do and he's going to try to take your life!"

Well, *that* got my attention. He went on to say, "Son, keep your prayer life up and you'll be fine. You're going to remember what I'm telling you. Now, I didn't come up here to frighten you but again I came to warn you! You're doing great things for the Lord and God's going to spare your life, but believe me, Satan doesn't like it at all so keep your guard up! You're going to be okay!"

The old man walked away and I never saw him again. I intended to ask Reverend Henson who he was and if he knew him but never had the chance that particular night. It seemed so random after such a great night with these folks to be approached in such a way, although he seemed very sincere as well as calm. In fact, he had a very peaceful countenance. But I've had a lot of people approach me after a concert and tell me some pretty amazing things "in the name of the Lord." Usually I would think that if it was true, then I'd have confirmation, or even more so their words would be confirmation of what God had already put in my mind or heart.

Memorial Day Weekend 2002

When our kids were growing up, one of my favorite things to do with them was to take a cross-country trip to California (which we did each summer for years). A day or so after the old preacher had approached me, I left on one of those trips with Holli, Haley, and my son Caleb—and quite honestly, I had totally forgotten what he said. Anyway, we were having a wonderful trip out west. I cherished my time with them as I'm gone so much of the time and I really do enjoy their company as well as their abilities to perform, which seems to be a blessing to other people as well. I also figured this would be our last family trip like this across the country since my daughters were getting all grown up!

We were at first scheduled to play at my friend Larry Thomas's church north of Los Angeles (Larry is now CEO of Fender Musical Instruments, then CEO of Guitar Center). After the service their worship leader asked to pray over the kids and me. He didn't pray the normal "God bless them on this trip . . . let them have a wonderful time" kind of thing but rather prayed several minutes for our protection and that God would send His angels to keep us and shelter us from harm. I remember thinking that the prayer was a bit different but I appreciated it nonetheless. We were also scheduled for a concert at one of our favorite churches in Southern California, The Packing House, which used to be a packing house in the middle of an orange grove in Redlands, California. Our friends Pastor Ed Rae and his wife "Rae-Rae"and the worship leader Ken Hutchcroft were some of our favorite folks to visit with. Their daughter Wendy was a big influence on Haley since she loved so much of the same kinds of music and fashion (which included 1940s stuff, believe it or not). There were hundreds of people at the church that night and we got three standing ovations. A number of our friends, such as Neal and Gwen Ferry and their entire family of about six or seven people, took a private jet out to the West Coast and came out to our concert. Our friends Paul and Graciela Rivera from Rivera Amplification came out as well.

We visited with these and other friends from that area for probably an hour and a half or so after our concert. Since it was so late, everyone just went their separate ways instead of going out for a meal afterward like we would often do. So the kids and I went to a local restaurant a short distance from the church.

We sat down, ordered our food, and were commenting on what a great time we'd just had. I thought how much I cherished this time with them. We had just gotten our food when we heard a commotion coming from the kitchen area and one of the dining areas a few yards away. I was appalled at the language and slamming of pots and pans and said to myself, "This is ridiculous to have such language and disturbance in a family restaurant like this! I'm definitely going to speak with the manager about this!" I turned around and saw a man lying on the floor in the foyer just a few yards away from us. We were in a booth and I had my back to the front door. I saw the cold steel black barrel of a shotgun being held to a man's head and at first I thought the police had chased someone down into the restaurant—but then my greatest fear came upon me. I slowly traced the gun barrel to the man holding it. He was dressed in black with a hood and a mask. They came in the restaurant with guns—my children there. This was not a good situation at all!

About that time the gunman started screaming, "All right, everybody stay down! I want your wallets . . . your cell phones . . . your purses!" Suddenly the music was turned off, and you couldn't hear anything but their obscene language as they made their hideous demands. It was easy to see now that the commotion we heard going on in the kitchen was one of the other robbers. In fact there were four masked men with guns and no doubt another outside who was the driver.

I turned back around and said to my kids, "Get down in your seats and let's pray right now!" It's hard to explain, but as I started praying it was as though an invisible covering was over our table. I sensed a strong witness of the Holy Spirit there with us. Still, I couldn't help but hear this debased man making his demands for the waitresses' tips and so on. Then it dawned on me that these men could pillage the place and take advantage of the women, including my daughters. I prayed, "Lord please, no matter what happens to me tonight . . . don't let these men touch my daughters!"

Suddenly I felt the cold reality that this could be the end for me.

Suddenly I felt the cold reality that this could be the end for me. I continued to pray and God's peace kept my heart and mind in Christ Jesus . . . and my family's too (Philippians 4:6–8).

Then I looked down and right next to me on the floor was the man who had been lying on the foyer floor. His leg was right beside me in front of our booth. I have no idea how he got there. I never heard him moving. The next thing I knew, this masked bandit told me to hand him my wallet. I looked at him and he got mad and told me not to look at him. He said, "Don't you look at me, boy!" My son Caleb never stopped looking at him and everything else going on, but no one was recognizable because of the face masks. He grabbed my wallet and said, "Man, you gotta have more than this!" I thought, *Oh no, my daughters always empty my wallet out for change for the merchandise table.* I never told him about the other money I had stashed under the credit cards since I figured he'd just take everything anyway, but he didn't. I cracked open my eyes looking downward enough that I could see the barrel of his shotgun under the table in my direction. The other man was still lying there on the floor next to him. I still didn't get that at all!

My daughter Holli said, "Sir, I have exactly what you need!" Then she handed him her Bible and he threw down his gun and was gloriously saved and we had dinner together! Hallelujah!!! OKAY NOT TRUE! Sorry for that but things don't always turn out as beautiful and perfect as we'd like just because we're believers. That actually wasn't the way it happened at all; however, it would've been a great story for my book! I wish I could say I heard angels singing and looked out the window and there were camels on the lawn and a huge light from heaven was shining right over our booth as I was praying! Wow!

But it wasn't that way either. These men were ruthless criminals and we heard later that they had been on a robbery rampage and had beaten up and even shot people in the wake of their destruction. This was a very hellacious attack against me and my family and although they didn't realize it, Satan had plotted the whole event.

My daughter Holli was actually too afraid to say anything and handed him the money bag from our CD sales. Then he quickly grabbed her cute little "Disney" wallet and took the few dollars she had. I thought, how despicable can a man get! My son Caleb just looked at him and shrugged his shoulders and said, "I don't have any money!" This world is sometimes so sick. What's strange is one minute we're getting a standing ovation and moments later we're in this surreal circumstance that could cause most people's hearts to shatter and ultimately put one into shock.

We continued to pray. I had shut my eyes in fear that this guy was going to shoot me. However, I looked down on the floor to see if the other man who was in the foyer before and whose leg pretty much covered the width of our booth was still there, but to my amazement he was gone! This guy was huge—how did he move away without me knowing it? I do remember seeing a Jesus logo on his shirt as he was lying there. Who was this dubious character? Was this guy an angel? Whoever he was . . . where was he?

Everything was quiet again right after the guy took our money. I think they got enough to appease them and then left. "THANK YOU JESUS!" The manager (who was also taken at gunpoint to the office safe) said, "They're gone—is everybody okay? Secure the doors . . . call the police!" All the waitresses started crying and screaming. There was such fear in that place but I looked at the kids and said, "Don't even go there! Let's stop right now and

SOMETIMES WHEN BIG SITUATIONS COME OUR WAY, WE JUST HAVE TO TRUST GOD AND RIDE THEM OUT!

just thank the Lord that a miracle took place tonight! No one is hurt! God is good!"

I don't think I'll ever forget this part—Caleb picked up his turkey burger and started to eat. The girls said, "Caleb, how in the world can you eat at a time like this?" (Caleb was thirteen and has always been real easy-going and laid-back.) He said, "Well, I'm not gonna let those guys ruin my meal! All they wanted to do is come in here and ruin everybody's meal!" He felt bad so he put his sandwich down. I said, "Come on, son, let's go to the restroom and wash up." I just felt dirty being around that sort of thing. We totally felt violated. As we were washing up, Caleb said to me, "Dad, I knew we were going to be okay. I did rededicate myself to God but I needed to do that anyway!" He cracked me up!

*Doyle's
2009 R. Taylor
Custom 12-string
"Short-Scale"
Figured African
Mahogany*

The way we all described the feelings we had during the robbery was that it felt as if we were going down on a plane. In other words, we felt helpless, as if we had no control. One moment I was asking my kids where they'd like to eat and I drove them over and we willingly walked in. Moments later we were completely at the mercy of terrible men. How did we wind up in such a situation?

This place was not a bar or late-night hang but a respectable family restaurant, not a place where you would ever suspect anything like this happening. But it did!

That night we stayed about an hour and a half away from where the robbery took place and called our family and friends. My old crooner buddy Johnny Tillotson and his wife, Nancy, had lunch with us the next day. We called our FBI buddy John Hall, and he called the other "Free Agents," a group of FBI men who are

MY FBI PAL AND FELLOW GUITAR PICKER, JOHN HALL AND ME IN STERLING, VA IN 2007.

highly trained "Agents" but sing like "Angels." One by one these wonderful friends called to cheer us up and give us prayer and moral support. John Hall told me that, statistically, the fact we survived uninjured (or worse) was rare. He said what I prayed God would protect the girls from normally happens in that situation. He said when there are several in a gang who rob a place, they normally would take their time and oftentimes do more than just take people's money.

I'm so thankful that God protected us. Honestly, the next day I could've hugged these terrible guys for not harming my family and me. We've all forgiven them in Jesus' name!

That night was a touchstone in my life in some important ways. I felt a peace and the presence of the Lord in the most adverse situation I'd ever been in. Like I said, it was like going down in a plane. I had absolutely no control over the situation — except they couldn't keep me from praying, and when I did I discovered God's peace is real. The only thing is you can't take a crash course in prayer in a situation like this. You're either connected or you're not! I'm so glad to know that I was and that God's peace really does pass all understanding.

Of course, my mind went back to the old man with the blue eyes just a little over a week before. I called my friend Brother Henson and asked about the old man. He said, "I was wondering who that fellow was. I've thought about him several times and you know, Doyle, I figured as long as I've been doing this and with all the people I've met and been personally acquainted with that I pretty much knew everyone in that room that night, but I honestly didn't know who he was. In fact, I don't think I'd ever seen him before. Just what did he say to you?" Then I told him (as Paul Harvey would've said) the rest of the story. He was in awe!

Recently I took Brother Henson to lunch. We talked again about the little old blue-eyed preacher and finally he said, "Well you know, Doyle, it would be just as easy to believe that he was an angel sent from the Lord to warn you."

Whoever he was, he hit the nail on the head, let me tell you. I'm glad I had some "light" on the subject. I'm thankful once again to be, as the old song says, "Walking in the Light of His Love." I saw the lights of God's love and protection for my family. I also experienced the Peace of God in a way that I never had before. Unlike the Marfa lights, this Peace is like an energy that can be felt and experienced even though it's not seen. But just like the Marfa lights, it's a reality that can't be explained except that it was the only thing Jesus said He would actually leave with us. The Marfa lights seem to have no purpose. The Peace that Jesus gives brings comfort and will keep our hearts and minds until we see Him face-to-face!

Favorite Scriptures for This Chapter

Isaiah 54:17

"'No weapon formed against you
shall prosper, and every tongue which rises
against you in judgment You shall condemn.
This is the heritage of the servants
of the LORD, and their righteousness
is from Me,' says the LORD."

Psalm 91

He who dwells in the secret place of the Most High
Shall abide under the shadow of the Almighty.
I will say of the LORD, "He is my refuge and my fortress;
My God, in Him I will trust."
Surely He shall deliver you from the snare of the fowler
And from the perilous pestilence.
He shall cover you with His feathers,
And under His wings you shall take refuge;
His truth shall be your shield and buckler.
You shall not be afraid of the terror by night,
Nor of the arrow that flies by day,
Nor of the pestilence that walks in darkness,
Nor of the destruction that lays waste at noonday.
A thousand may fall at your side,
And ten thousand at your right hand;
But it shall not come near you.

Only with your eyes shall you look,

And see the reward of the wicked.

Because you have made the LORD, who is my refuge,

Even the Most High, your dwelling place,

No evil shall befall you,

Nor shall any plague come near your dwelling;

For He shall give His angels charge over you,

To keep you in all your ways.

In their hands they shall bear you up,

Lest you dash your foot against a stone.

You shall tread upon the lion and the cobra,

The young lion and the serpent you shall trample underfoot.

Because he has set his love upon Me,

therefore I will deliver him;

I will set him on high, because he has known My name.

He shall call upon Me, and I will answer him;

I will be with him in trouble;

I will deliver him and honor him.

With long life I will satisfy him,

And show him my salvation.

Ephesians 6:10–17

Finally, my brethren, be strong in the Lord
and in the power of His might.
Put on the whole armor of God, that you may
be able to stand against the wiles of the devil.
For we do not wrestle against flesh and blood,
but against principalities, against powers, against the rulers
of the darkness of this age, against spiritual hosts of wickedness
in the heavenly places. Therefore take up
the whole armor of God, that you may be able to withstand
in the evil day, and having done all, to stand.
Stand therefore, having girded your waist with truth,
having put on the breastplate of righteousness,
and having shod your feet with the preparation of
the gospel of peace; above all, taking the shield of faith
with which you will be able to quench all the
fiery darts of the wicked one. And take the helmet
of salvation, and the sword of the Spirit,
which is the word of God.

John 16:33

"These things I have spoken to you,
that in Me you may have peace.
In the world you will have tribulation;
but be of good cheer,
I have overcome the world."

*Doyle Deluxe model
(DDX) Taylor guitar*

CHAPTER 14

The Changing of the Guard

It was March of 1998 and my first time ever going to Europe. I was playing at the Music Messe in Frankfurt, Germany, which is the equivalent of our NAMM (music manufacturers') show for Europe and pretty much the rest of the world. Music Messe is a huge event, and people come from all over the world to attend this incredible show, which was then managed by my good friend Dr. Michael Peters. I was playing at different booths, sort of like I did in the early years at NAMM going from booth to booth from the vendors I represented, such as Taylor Guitars, Rivera Amplifiers, and GHS Strings. There were no stages; I would play at the edge of the aisles and I was thankful that people would gather around. It was great fun.

I especially remember one fellow who showed up nearly every time I played. For some reason, I couldn't help but notice him. Although he was not in uniform, I figured he was an American soldier. After my last song on one of my "stops," I motioned for him to come over so I could speak with him. I said, "Okay, you're one of us, aren't you? Are you in the army?"

He said, "Is it that obvious? Was it the haircut?" He also told me he was a guitar player, which I already figured. I told him how much I appreciated him for being there across the ocean for our country. He told me how much he appreciated my music, which made me feel great. He said he was on leave just to come over to the show because he loved music and had heard a lot about the Music Messe. He was stationed in Bosnia at the time and was a tank platoon commander for the US Army. He was First Sergeant Aaron D. Jagger.

Doyle's 2004 Taylor 30th Anniversary Koa

Before he left I simply told him I would be praying for him and gave him each of my CDs and some thumb picks. I didn't get into a deep conversation about the Lord, but it was quite evident that I was a Christian. I had played songs there such as "The Lord's Prayer," "Amazing Grace," and "How Great Thou Art," along with my fast finger-picking tunes. (It was amazing how quiet things got when I started playing the sacred songs.) He came back later with a friend he wanted me to meet, Sergeant Matthew Creath. He was also stationed in Bosnia and was a guitar player as well, and they actually played music together. I loaded him down with stuff too.

I guess my music has now been played in battlefields around the world, so I have been told. As some of you know, I typically open all of my shows with a medley of patriotic songs and always mention our troops around the world and how we should remember them and pray for them every day, which I also do.

SERGEANT FIRST CLASS MATTHEW CREATH. I BELIEVE WE WERE IN GERMANY HERE. AS YOU CAN SEE HE LOVES GUITARS AS MUCH AS ME. (2000)

About a month after I returned home, I got this letter from Sergeant Jagger. He told me what an impression my music had made on his life as well as my testimony and telling him that I would pray for him. He went on to say that the days following, he got under conviction about his lifestyle and asked God to forgive him and then called his wife and asked if she would forgive him and if they could get back together. He said she forgave him and they got back together again as a family. They had five daughters.

I could hardly believe what I was reading! It was like a country music song played backward . . . he got his wife back, the kids back, the dog back, and his guitar pickin' back! He told me that his life was changed since that day we met in Germany. I was completely amazed and delighted!

The next year at the Music Messe, Sergeant Matthew Creath came to the show, but his friend Sergeant Jagger wasn't able to be there. However, it was great to see Matthew doing well and also knowing that he had rededicated his heart to the Lord as well. Matthew told me how they were playing at church together and using their gifts for the Lord. These guys had become heroes of mine, and I appreciated their friendship.

All day long I had this tune in my head that was sort of a sad, wailing melody.

On the day following the trade show, I got in the backseat of a Volkswagen Passat and rode from Frankfurt, Germany, through Switzerland, and up to Lake Como, Italy. In the front seat were two of my close friends, Paul Rivera (who I've talked about before) and David Magagna, who at that time was the International Director for Taylor Guitars. I listened to them talk and tell funny "war stories" of their experiences in the music business. However, my mind was on my two soldier friends and the miracle of their life-changing experience in the Lord and how it all started by coming to the Music Messe. All day long I had this tune in my head that was sort of a sad, wailing melody. I was writing this song in my head as I often do, and I knew it was going to be special.

When we got to the hotel at Lake Como late that night, I said good night to the guys and before I even found the lights of my bedroom, I opened the blinds to look out the window. It literally took my breath away! I had no idea how beautiful it was there. You could see the moonlight on the lake as well as its reflection on the magnificent snow-capped Alps of Switzerland in the background. It was one of the most spectacular views I've ever encountered, and I've seen some pretty amazing spots around the world! Our hotel was directly on the lake. In fact, you could look straight down into the water if you hung your head out of the window.

I began to feel around for my guitar case in the room and very quietly began to play for the first time the melody and chords that had been in my head all day. I didn't write this song, really, but like so many others I just played them for the first time. I was playing this song all the way through and when I got to the end, the most beautiful ending came to me. In fact, it was so pretty, I started to weep. This has only happened a few times in my life. Another time was when I wrote "The Visitation," of course, and there was also one I wrote in Champaign, Illinois, called "Passings."

It was late one night after a gig in Champaign, and although I was tired, I just felt like playing a little bit before I went to bed. I sensed a very sad feeling in the air. I began to play this sad melody. Again, it just flowed like I was playing something familiar — but yet it was brand-new. I also sat and wept after I played it. My daughter Holli was with me. I told her I felt very sad, like someone

OFTENTIMES A MELODY WILL JUST COME INTO MY HEAD, EVEN BEFORE I GET A CHANCE TO PLAY IT ON THE GUITAR. IT SORT OF HANGS AROUND IN MY MIND UNTIL IT BECOMES A SONG. AND THEN IT GOES AWAY!

had died. She also said how beautiful she felt the song was, and maybe the Lord gave it to me for a reason. People often ask how I remember a song when I don't write anything down. I heard it best described by my friend Tommy Emmanuel. "If it's a song, then how can you forget it?" It's true! It just lingers on in your mind, but normally when it's finished and all the parts and the arrangements are all done, it goes out of your head until you play it again.

When I got up the next morning, I picked up my guitar and started to play. The song was still there. Later that day, I found out that my friend Randy Hauser (drummer for Chet Atkins) had died suddenly as well as a wonderful pastor friend in California, Bill Stuthridge, who also passed away unexpectedly that same day. Later I recorded this song in California with my favorite arranger and conductor Tom Keene and orchestra. It's about seven or eight minutes long. I've heard of people playing it at funeral services and memorials. It's on my Windham Hill / BMG album, *Gitarre 2000* (German spelling for guitar).

The next morning in Lake Como, Italy, I played the song for David and Paul and told them I had been hearing it in my head since we left Frankfurt the day before. I also told them about Aaron and Matthew and how their lives were changed and how God put Aaron's family back together again. Paul Rivera is a very emotional man, and he was very moved just hearing about it. I told them I wanted to call the song "The Changing of the Guard" because of how God intervened and changed their lives.

Some months later, I got word from Sergeant Creath that he was retiring, and that Aaron Jagger had been transferred to a training facility in north Georgia, which was a short distance from my home in Cleveland, Tennessee. So far this was the story: we met in Germany, his life was changed, he got his family back, and now he's living twenty-five miles away from us. Isn't that strange!

I managed to get a number to his office and when he got on the phone he couldn't believe it was me because he had no idea I was that close to him either. I invited him to accompany me to a prayer breakfast sponsored by a church a few miles west of Atlanta, which was about two hours away.

I picked up Sergeant Jagger about five o'clock in the morning, and as we were on our trip, I told him about writing "The Changing of the Guard" and how it was going to be on my next CD. I had also recorded this song with Tom Keene and a string orchestra. I had made him a copy of the studio mix, and he seemed amazed and excited. I was thrilled to be able to share this music with him that he and his buddy Matthew had inspired. On the trip he also told me how he wanted to be involved in ministry and how he and his wife were planning their civilian futures around that. He wanted to go to a Bible college in Chattanooga, Tennessee. He also told me that he'd been writing a lot of songs and wanted to record a CD someday and use his talent for God. I asked if he would sing a song during my program that morning. It was a special "Resurrection Breakfast" with a couple hundred men having breakfast, sharing testimonies, and fellowshipping together. I was the morning entertainment and speaker.

Doyle's 2010 Taylor Custom Solid Body Walnut

I'll never forget that service. I had already played a few songs and then told the story of how we had met in Germany and so on and how I wrote a song for him and his buddy Matthew Creath. I asked him to come up and sing a song. Well, he was not just pretty good . . . Aaron was GREAT! Everybody loved

He was truly a warrior, a brave courageous soldier.

him, so I asked him to do another, and then another. Finally I just asked if he would give his testimony. That was all it took. That morning, men's lives were touched and changed forever after listening to the testimony of First Sergeant Aaron Jagger, the soldier, the father, and the man of God.

On our two-hour drive back home, Aaron then told me what he did in his military career. He also told me how good he was at blowing things up like bridges and buildings and what devastation one tank could do. Some things he told me were almost unimaginable as I'd never heard of such destructive power from a weapon such as this. It was almost as if I was sitting there talking to a mastermind of destruction. Well actually, he was just that. He was truly a warrior, a brave courageous soldier. Before he left, he told me more about his plans after retirement (which wasn't that far off). Then he said if anything happened again in a war situation, they probably would not allow him to retire.

This was shortly before September 11, 2001. Aaron was ultimately sent to Iraq.

During Aaron's tour of duty in Iraq, he was still playing his guitar and singing as well as teaching others how to play. He formed a band in his company called The Bandits and was the guitarist and vocalist of the group. They performed often at memorial services for fallen soldiers. He also shared his testimony and faith in the Lord Jesus Christ.

Through the years I've also seen my friend Matthew Creath, who continues to play his guitar and is greatly involved at his local church with his family back at his home in Virginia. It was Matthew who told me that on August 9, 2006, Aaron and two fellow soldiers were killed by a roadside bomb, also commonly called an IED (improvised explosive device), in Ramadi, Iraq. He was forty-three years old. Aaron didn't fight in the war because he hated the enemy but because he loved his country.

In 1998, at a very busy and noisy music trade show with thousands of people pushing and shoving and moving down the aisles, First Sergeant Aaron D. Jagger saw the lights of Forgiveness, Restoration, and Peace . . . and he was changed! Through time, I saw the lights of God's Amazing Grace and the Power of His love, which is the greatest power of all. It is powerful enough to change the lives of men for all eternity — where I believe Aaron is now playing his guitar in the presence of the Lord . . . The Changing of the Guard.

To hear Doyle play "The Changing of the Guard,"
pop in your DVD or go to

www.doyledykes.com/tlom.htm

To hear Doyle talk about what goes through his mind
when he plays a song like "White Rose for Heidi" or
"Changing of the Guard," pop in your DVD or go to

www.doyledykes.com/tlom.htm

FAVORITE SCRIPTURES FOR THIS CHAPTER

John 15:13
"Greater love has no one than this,
than to lay down one's life for his friends."

Matthew 5:14–16
"You are the light of the world. A city that is set
on a hill cannot be hidden. Nor do they light a lamp
and put it under a basket, but on a lampstand,
and it gives light to all who are in the house. Let your
light so shine before men, that they may see your
good works and glorify your Father in heaven."

Romans 8:1
"There is therefore now no condemnation to
those who are in Christ Jesus, who do not walk
according to the flesh, but according to the Spirit."

Romans 8:34–39
"Who is he who condemns? It is Christ who died,
and furthermore is also risen, who is even at the
right hand of God, who also makes intercession
for us. Who shall separate us from the
love of Christ? Shall tribulation, or distress,
or persecution, or famine, or nakedness,
or peril, or sword? As it is written:

'For Your sake we are killed all day long;
we are accounted as sheep for the slaughter.'
Yet in all these things we are more than
conquerors through Him who loved us.
For I am persuaded that neither death nor life,
nor angels nor principalities nor powers,
nor things present nor things to come,
nor height nor depth, nor any other created thing,
shall be able to separate us from the love of God
which is in Christ Jesus our Lord."

Second Corinthians 5:17
"Therefore, if anyone is in Christ,
he is a new creation; old things have passed away;
behold, all things have become new."

John 6:37
"All that the Father gives Me
will come to Me, and the one who comes to Me
I will by no means cast out."

TUNING FOR "THE CHANGING OF THE GUARD"

CGDGBE

CHAPTER 15

My Personal British Invasion

If you were around during the 1960s, you'll remember that the whole Beatles experience blew across the Atlantic like a tidal wave directly from the shores of England. Their hairstyles, their fashionable clothes, their pointed boots, their unusual guitars (they played German instruments like Paul's Hofner bass, and they made the American-made Rickenbacker 12-string famous) and VOX amplifiers, and their English accents set them apart from any other entertainers—including Elvis. AM radio was huge, and WAPE in Jacksonville, Florida, (The Big Ape) aired their music most all of the time. Plus, they had just played on the *Ed Sullivan Show*, and that was about as incredible as life could get.

But as you know by now, I was raised in a conservative Christian home and our entire lives were centered around our church, so to us the Beatles were like aliens from another planet. The closest thing to us seeing a "foreigner" where I grew up was watching a group of French sailors walking down the street while in port from the shipyards a few blocks from our house. Europe wasn't merely another country or continent . . . to us it was like going to the moon! So even though a lot of people thought they were cool and talented, my folks wouldn't have any part of their revolution. We felt they were infidels without God and without any real purpose.

The thought came to me that I was forty-four years old and had never owned a Beatles album.

It shouldn't surprise you that my dad wasn't past having a little fun at their expense. I remember gas stations with their "gas wars" offering a black-and-white photo of the band and a cheesy molded plastic "Beatle wig" with every fill-up. Even though he didn't seem to care for their music, he couldn't pass that up—he would take all our guests into the kitchen where he would jokingly show them the Beatles' photo tacked inside the cabinet, explaining how it would "keep the beetles out of the cabinet." Then he would put on that old cheap-looking plastic wig that he got from the gas station. It was awful looking but he thought it was funny. We all did!

That's why we didn't pay too much attention when the Beatles came to Jacksonville on September 11, 1964—which was the day after Hurricane Dora hit our city. They still played to 23,000 people in 45 mph winds at the Gator Bowl—but we were more focused on dealing with the cleanup after the storm. We went without electricity for several days and actually stayed at our church since they'd opened it up as a storm shelter. It almost seemed eerie how such a violent storm hit our community at the same time the most popular rock band in the world came to our city.

Now, let's move up to 1998. The thought came to me that I was forty-four years old and had never owned a Beatles album. I had just performed a concert in St. Petersburg, Florida, and was on my way home. I was trying to make it past the Georgia line as I was on my way home for a couple of days and anxious to see my family. The only thing was, I was so obsessed by not having ever owned a Beatles album that I pulled over to an all-night Walmart store in Lake City, Florida, and circled the parking lot about midnight. Then I decided that I obviously needed a "support group" and got back on the interstate, on my way home once again.

However, I was determined that I would buy every Beatles CD available and catch up on what I'd missed out on all those years.

The next afternoon I met my family for dinner in Chattanooga a few miles away from our home. After dinner I took my family to a local record store. We all sort of meandered about doing our own thing, except one of my daughters helped me locate the Fab Four, and soon I had an armload of the Beatles' CDs and was looking for Rita to go to the cash register. Just then I got a call on my cell phone. It was my producer Larry Hamby from Windham Hill / BMG Records in California. He said, "Hey Doyle, we're putting together a compilation album of all Beatles songs called *Here, There and Everywhere,* and I've recommended that you find one of your favorites and record it for the album."

There I was holding two armloads of Beatles records (or CDs) and for a moment I was speechless. I was looking around

Doyle's 1964 Gretsch Chet Atkins 6120 (a gift from Harvey Simmons)

for the cameras that obviously were feeding him live video to his Beverly Hills office of our retro-rocket descent back to the '60s to invade the British! Was it funny . . . or weird? It was surreal indeed, as the timing almost proved to have been a phenomenal coincidence.

All I could say was, WOW! Mr. Hamby asked, "Are you okay with this?" I said, "Yes . . . I'm thinking I'm fine with it." As it turned out, the album had some wonderful musicians such as George Winston, Tuck and Patti, Wayne Johnson, and the late Michael Hedges. The song I chose was "Girl," mainly because it was my daughter Holli's favorite. It also ended up on my *Gitarre 2000* CD on that same label.

But now I had a struggle. Given my upbringing, how could this be from the Lord? Was I finally selling out my heritage and my convictions? What made it harder was that my kids were listening to these aliens and wondered how they came up with such unique and catchy songs. They all loved them!

It was a year or so later after my solo album had been released on Windham Hill and I was performing at the Florida Theatre in my hometown of Jacksonville, Florida. The theatre people had arranged for an interview with the local NPR station and I asked my dad "Bubba" (that's what everyone except me called him) to come along with me. I took my guitar and played a little and we talked about the show at the theatre as well as the new record being released on Windham Hill. They also mentioned the compilation album of the Beatles songs, *Here, There and Everywhere,* and asked how I came up with the song "Girl" as my selection. I explained the story of never owning a Beatles album when I was young because my parents didn't allow me to have one.

They looked at my dad and asked him if that were true and why. It was an absolute golden moment in my life. Here's my dad and me on a very popular radio show, hearing the question as to why he had allowed me to be so deprived of owning a simple Beatles record like all my other friends at school. I'm sure they were thinking of all those pent-up years of my being so underprivileged and how could he do such a thing. The truth was, I didn't really care or know any better at the time. My heroes were guitar guys and by the time I had money to buy a record, I couldn't wait for the next Chet Atkins or Merle Travis record to come out. But boy, was I enjoying this moment!

They asked him again: "Is that right, Mr. Dykes, you didn't allow Doyle to even own a Beatles record?" He said, "Well, those boys were really good musicians and I liked their music! I even have a couple of Beatles records myself!"

I said, "WHAT? All these years and you never said anything about the Beatles!"

"Well, you know . . . they were real different with their long hair and all, but they were really great musicians. I liked their songs!"

Oh my goodness! My father on the radio exposed his true feelings regardless of my deprived and disadvantaged childhood. It was such a wonderful tongue-in-cheek moment and I'll never forget it.

Given the unique beginning of my Beatles experience with the CDs in the store and my contribution to a Beatles' compilation CD on a major label, I was pretty satisfied that my "British Invasion" experience was over. It wasn't over by a long shot!

The Cavern Club

In the fall of 1999 I took another trip to Great Britain with my friends at Sound Technology. The owner, Robert Wilson, had offered to personally take us to our performances, along with a small entourage from his company. The compelling force behind all this was more than money and selling guitars. I could sense these guys loved music and loved the whole idea of exposing me to their culture as well as introducing their folks to my music. It was also interesting to me to see how great of an impact the Beatles had on these guys, since they were from their home turf.

It was a typical cold, blustery afternoon in the city of Liverpool when we arrived at the Adelphi Hotel, only blocks away from the Mersey River. (Remember the song "Ferry across the Mersey"?) The Adelphi was a famous hotel that was built in 1826 but remodeled in 1912 to accommodate the passengers of the large cruise liners, especially those of the White Star Line — primarily, the *Titanic*. In fact, the Sefton Suite in the hotel is an exact replica of the smoking lounge of the *Titanic*. We were told it was actually designed by the same man.

Of course this room was huge and more like a ballroom. I had afternoon tea with the guys there in that beautiful room. Ironically, even the doors of the hotel rooms opened backward like those on a ship. Liverpool was much like my hometown of Jacksonville, since the shipyards were in the heart of the city. The old international customs and international trade buildings were no doubt previously the heart of this beautiful metropolitan city.

When we got to the venue, I walked down the cold black stairs lined on both sides with posters of famous music stars to the catacomb-like spaces with archways connecting several rooms. The stage was lined with Taylor guitars, and the sound engineer was eagerly waiting for my sound check. It typically doesn't take me long for a sound check, so I just sort of milled around the place until showtime.

I was nervous. One reason for this was the fact that I didn't usually play clubs and here I was in the most famous one in the entire world: the Cavern Club . . . Birthplace of the Beatles!

I'll never forget going into the men's room way in the back behind the stage and taking my Amplified Bible out of my hip pocket and turning to Philippians 4:13, "I have strength for all things in Christ Who empowers me [I am ready for anything and equal to anything through Him Who infuses inner strength into me; I am self-sufficient in Christ's sufficiency]." I specifically remember saying this prayer: "Lord, You know I didn't ask to be here but I was 'asked' to be here so please, Lord, I ask You in the Name of Jesus—just show up."

Shortly thereafter, I was introduced and played my heart out for a couple of hours. Things were going very well, and then I really stuck my neck out and said, "You know, I believe music is a gift from God and you don't have to 'expand your mind' with drugs or excessive alcohol to put yourself into a state of creativity. God created the gift of music and He put that creative spirit in us. I realize where I am tonight and that the most popular musicians and songwriters in the world have stood in this very spot!" Then, I introduced the song "How Great Thou Art," and the Lord really blessed it. In other words, He showed up. His presence filled that dungeonlike edifice. It was as powerful as any church service I'd ever played at. The crowd went crazy. I sensed the presence of the Holy Spirit in a very strong way. Even Robert Wilson and the guys from Sound Technology acknowledged that something very special happened at the Cavern Club that evening.

As I was leaving the stage, the manager of the club, Ray Johnson, ran over and grabbed me by the arm and started leading me out of the building. I thought to myself, *Oh well, I guess I've done it now. I got preachy again and this time I said way too much!* Typically I take time with the audience and sign things and meet people but he was taking me out of the place. He said, "Hey, I need to get you out of here. I want to show you something and I think you're going to like this!" He continued, "We loved your music and the way you play that guitar. It's the real deal and I can tell you're from Tennessee . . . but the things you said tonight— we've never heard words like this before!"

Then, he took me outside to the front of the building and showed me the "Wall of Fame" — bricks that had names inscribed in each of them. The centerpiece of the wall was a plaque describing the wall and its purpose and a bit of the history of the Cavern.

Around the plaque were the names of musicians and bands such as the Beatles, of course, with a brick for John, Paul, George, and Ringo, and then others like Oasis, Chuck Berry, the Rolling Stones, John Lee Hooker, the Hollies, the Shadows, Stevie Wonder, and many more. He explained the entire idea of the Wall of Fame and how it began. He also explained that the people who were honored were not only people who had played at the Cavern, but that they also made a "mark" or influence on the people through their performances there.

I thought he was taking me out of the place to scold or ridicule me— instead he honored me.

I thought it was very interesting but unusual that he took me there at the time he did, right as I was about to meet the folks there. It was almost as if he couldn't wait to tell me about it. Then, he looked me right in the eyes and said, "We all agree that you deserve to have your name up there too!"

I couldn't believe my ears. I thought he was taking me out of the place to scold or ridicule me—instead he honored me. There was actually no "invasion" but an "invitation" into this world that had always seemed so foreign to me in more ways than one. This was so far beyond my thoughts it's hard to describe even to this very day (Ephesians 3:20).

The next day before we left, we were taken on a bus tour called "the Magical Mystery Tour," which was owned by the same people who now own the Cavern Club. The tour took us to the childhood homes of John Lennon, Paul McCartney, George Harrison, and

Ringo Starr and to some of the places that inspired their songs, such as Eleanor Rigby's home and church, and Strawberry Fields (which was a private school). We could see everything Paul McCartney was seeing when he penned the song "Penny Lane" as we rode down that very street—such as the fish and chips shop, the bank, and the fire station. It was actually quite enjoyable. We saw the humble beginnings where these "kids" would get together and write songs . . . the songs that took America and the rest of the world by storm.

I also saw the place where John's mother was killed by a car as she was crossing the road after visiting her son at the home of her sister, "Mimi," who raised John as her own son. I never knew this until I was at the very place where it happened. You never know where people come from and what they've gone through in life.

Oh yes, I remember the controversial words of John Lennon about Christianity and the Beatles being "more popular" than Jesus Christ. He apologized for that later, but the damage was done to many of us Bible-belters in the South. This caused such a disturbance that there were record burnings and their images were burned in effigy. I would be a

THE MANAGER/OWNER OF THE CAVERN CLUB, RAY JOHNSON, AND ME AT THE WALL OF FAME IN 2000. HE SAID THEY RELOCATED IT IN THE CENTER OF THE WALL AT A LATER DATE. UNBELIEVABLE!

hypocrite if I said I would've done any better. Recently while watching the movie *Amazing Grace*, I was brought to tears by John Newton's statement, "I'm a great sinner and Christ is a great Savior!" Where would any of us be if not for the Grace of God?

It's funny but this all happened while their music was simple and innocent, which was my favorite era—even though by the late '60s some of their music became more drug-influenced.

A few years ago I was playing at a large church, and a gospel musician I really appreciated came up to me after the service and reminded me of the disgraceful words of Lennon. He raked me over the coals and rebuked me for playing and recording a song by the Beatles. Should I have accepted his rebuke and asked God to forgive me? I remembered the words of my old Welsh pastor friend "Uncle Arthur Burt" and how he once responded to a similar situation by saying, "I appreciate that, but I don't have to answer to you but to Him!" So I apologized if I offended him but also explained how God was using their songs to catch the attention of people so I could share the truth with them.

I can't tell you how many musicians I know who have been influenced by the Beatles, or even how many pastors were huge Beatles' fans growing up. I've even been asked to play Beatles' songs in outreach crusades such as George Harrison's "While My Guitar Gently Weeps" simply because people loved these songs and we could get their attention and then share the gospel. I can only imagine how great an impact these guys could've made the kingdom of God and how much good could've been done. I personally don't believe they had a clue, in their early years especially, how powerful they were. Same with the British bands that followed them, such as the Rolling Stones, Led Zeppelin, Cream, Pink Floyd, Free, and many more. Instead of simply condemning these guys, wouldn't it have been better if a more positive statement was made to the Beatles by the Christian community? Instead of burning their records and their images, perhaps they could've reached out to them and said something like, "I hope you guys will someday experience Christ in your life and the difference only He can make. He'll change your heart and give you that peace you seem to be trying to attain. That's His specialty because He's the Prince of Peace. Jesus is also King of kings and Lord of lords and of His kingdom, there shall be no end. Christianity is here to stay and we're not talking about Christianity as a mere religion, but as having a relationship with God through His Son Jesus Christ."

Let's make that statement now. Today. Music is still one of the most powerful tools on earth to make a statement. Let's pray for the pop, rock, country, blues, jazz, and all entertainers that they'll receive Christ and promote truth!

It was a year after I played the Cavern Club that I was invited back for the official unveiling of my brick in the Wall of Fame. My wife, Rita, and daughter Heidi and son Caleb were also there to share the experience with me. Once again Robert Wilson escorted us around and was a most gracious host. I felt sort of like a rock star!

Since then I've been back to England many times. I've played in theatres and many ballrooms, including the beautiful ballroom at the Savoy Hotel. I've played on the BBC in England on the *Big George* show, which is one of the most popular in the UK. On a tour for Taylor Guitars and Sound Technology only weeks after 9/11/2001, I was playing for a thousand people—two different shows—and I felt something move me to tell them that it wasn't a time for us to shrink up or shrivel up but to stretch out and play to as many people as possible and use our God-given gifts. I refused to let terrorism take away my gift and my calling.

Here I was making this decree to a country where terrorism is always at the door. However, I believe it was just at the right time as there were a number of threats there as well even on the streets outside our hotel.

One other "Beatles experience" happened when I stayed in a small hotel called the Regent in Doncaster, England, where "the boys" once stayed. The room had never been redecorated. Even the drapes and wallpaper had never been changed. There were still the same four small beds in the room. The Beatles had just hit the charts and had to be carried away secretly in an armored truck to divert the crowds. The hotel people told me that the night the Beatles stayed there they had opened the show for Roy Orbison, and the story goes he wouldn't allow them to open for him again. They had become the big draw, although the Beatles so admired Roy Orbison and were no doubt thrilled to be onstage with him. However, that night was the last time they opened a show for him or anyone else. Cool experience!

I've also been to Knebworth House, which was the largest rock venue in Europe, hosting festivals with the Rolling Stones, Pink Floyd, Led Zeppelin, and even the boys from Jacksonville, Lynyrd Skynyrd, who were a huge hit at Knebworth. Lord Henry Lytton Cobbold and his lovely wife, Martha, and their family have been a blessing to me. The estate has been in his family since 1491. I wrote a song for their house called "Knebworth Dream," featured on their DVD for their house tours. I recorded it in their five-hundred-year-old barn, which is now a studio. I made a DVD called *Live Sessions* and taped "Knebworth Dream" in the same room where Michael Keaton and Kim Basinger were in the dining hall as it was portrayed as Bruce Wayne Manor in the movie *Batman*. Winston Churchill had painted a picture of the room and it was displayed behind me. Knebworth House was one of his favorite places to visit.

I also recorded a song I wrote for Robert Wilson's home and especially dedicated it to his wife, Mary, called "At Swangleys Farm." Each year I play at their local church just down the road for the Evensong service. In the beginning there were only a few people, but each year it has grown to a full house of people who even come up from London, many of whom are involved in the music industry. So God has blessed me with friendships and opportunities that I never dreamed I would ever see.

I've also been to Scotland and Ireland many times. The first time I went to Belfast, I was in a hotel lobby just across the street from the airport. The concierge approached me and asked quietly, "The manager thinks she recognizes you. Could you please tell me your name?" I told him and he responded, "Who, sir? Okay, thanks, I'll tell her." My daughter Haley asked what he wanted and I told her that he thought the manager had recognized me. She thought that was pretty cool since we'd never been to Belfast before. However, I told her I believed they thought I was someone else. She said, "Oh Dad, they probably saw you on that musician channel or something."

I said, "No, Haley, I believe they thought I was Meat Loaf." I've actually gotten that before. She insisted they knew who I was!

A few minutes later we were driven downtown to the Belfast BBC (British Broadcasting Company) radio studios. As we were on our way, Haley burst into laughter in the taxi. I asked what on earth was so funny and she pointed to a huge sign on the side of a building that said, "Meat Loaf Is Coming to Belfast!"

That night as we were leaving the venue (ironically in front of the docks where the *Titanic* was built), the taxi driver randomly turned to the host of our event and asked, "Isn't that Doyle Dykes the guitar player?" When they told me that later, I didn't believe them. In fact, I didn't believe them for a couple of days. It was told to me that a UK channel called Sky TV had been running some videos of me. Astonishing!

For several days some people had warned us not to talk about "religion" in Belfast. In fact, so many people had mentioned it that Haley got worried about it and I told her how my old friend Rev. Danny Drake (a pastor I had worked with in the '80s) once told me that the Holy Spirit was a gentleman and that He knows how to work in the right situation without offending people.

That's not to diminish the work of the Holy Spirit to convict, but it is His work—not ours. I told Haley to "just be yourself," as I was going to do, and the Lord would take care of the rest.

When we got into the studio of the BBC, the afternoon deejay was a most interesting-looking chap. He had tattoos and piercings and that cool Irish musical accent and had the energy of a teenager. "All right, Doyle, you've played U2, and Grand Ole Opry stuff . . . we heard you also play sacred music on the guitar. What's that like?" Haley looked at me and cracked a smile, and I said we'll be glad to show you. I didn't say a word but just began to play "Amazing Grace" and He showed up once again but this time on national radio that was broadcast all over Ireland. Haley began to sing and when we finished, the deejay was rubbing his arms as he said, "Whoa . . . That was very fantastic. I wish you people could feel what I feel in the studio today!" He had goose bumps all over his tattoos and you could definitely sense the presence of the Lord there that day.

Through my personal British invasion, I saw the reality that these "aliens" called the Beatles were really just kids whose outlet in life was music—just like mine was. They even came from the same kind of port city. I saw the lights of forgiveness toward these musicians whom I'd never met but who had influenced me in my guitar playing. And I've made lifelong friends who live in castles and farmhouses; I've played to kids who have lived a lifetime by the time they've reached their late teens. They stole my heart.

Because of the impact these folks have made on my family, even my grandson's name is William Lennon Brown—known as "Lenny." The British "invaded" my life, and I'll always be grateful for that intrusion.

To watch Doyle play "Birmingham Steele,"
which he started writing in Tennessee but finished
when he got to England, pop in your DVD or go to
www.doyledykes.com/tlom.htm

Some of My Favorite British Experiences

Camden Market; Knebworth House; the Lake District and Chatsworth;
the city of Bath; York; Cambridge; the Borders and
the Highlands of Scotland; Devon County; the music district of Dublin;
Belfast; London and the theatres in the West End.

Favorite Scriptures for This Chapter

Philippians 4:13
"I have strength for all things in Christ Who
empowers me [I am ready for anything and equal to
anything through Him Who infuses inner strength into me;
I am self-sufficient in Christ's sufficiency]." (AMP)

Matthew 7:3–5
"And why do you look at the speck in your brother's eye,
but do not consider the plank in your own eye?
Or how can you say to your brother, 'Let me remove
the speck from your eye'; and look, a plank is in your own eye?
First remove the plank from your own eye, and then you
will see clearly to remove the speck from your brother's eye."

Doyle's 1995 Taylor Custom Presentation Brazilian

CHAPTER 16

A Compassionate Friend

On December 23, 2004, I had surgery for a brain tumor called an "acoustic neuroma." I think it was Bob Taylor who said I should title my next album after that. (Sometimes you just have to laugh!) Although it was benign it still had to be removed.

The procedure I chose was my only choice in order to have a fifty-fifty chance to keep my hearing on my right side. If I had simply sacrificed my hearing, I could've taken a much less critical approach for removal. As a musician especially, I felt I had to at least try to retain my hearing. I love stereo!

I remember waking up after surgery and seeing my wife, Rita, and brother, Aubrey, and friends Duane and Deed Eddy. They looked to me as if they were spinning around in a funnel. That's because the procedure meant my surgeon had to compress my brain, which left me with terrible residual effects such as extreme headaches with accompanying nausea that could only be described as unbearable. I also lost my sense of balance as this type of tumor attaches itself to the balance nerve. I had to learn to walk again. I also ultimately lost the hearing on my right side, which was the very thing I had tried to preserve. The surgeon told me he felt it was due to a lack of blood flow. After all, the Bible says in Leviticus 17:11, "The life of the flesh is in the blood" (KJV).

It's taken several years to finally get over the headaches. I still battle them pretty much daily, but the severe ones have eased. If you view my DVD *Live Sessions*, you'll see me playing in England at a beautiful stately home called Knebworth House. I was so sick that day! I had been throwing up for hours and could play the song I wrote for the house, "Knebworth Dream," only one time through. I made it through the outdoor interviews and then quickly ran over and threw up in Lord Henry's flower garden. As I did many times before when I'd get this sick, I called my little mama in Florida and she'd pray me through to healing.

That's a story I'll have to tell another time, but it's certainly the reason for receiving a call in February of 2006 from one of my guitar heroes, Mr. Eric Johnson. He had apologized for not coming out to my concert a couple of nights before when I was in his hometown of Austin, Texas. We small-talked a bit, and then he asked how I was doing physically and how my ear was. I explained that I still didn't have any hearing in my right side but that the good things definitely outweighed the bad things, and I was thrilled to still be doing what I loved. And that, of course, is playing my guitar and making music around the world.

He told me that he had spoken to a friend of ours who did come out to my concert and how he had mentioned to him about my wanting to try out an overdrive effects pedal to add to my pedal board for my guitar. This is such a random thought anyway, as most acoustic guitar players don't use overdrive type pedals (that's because they distort the sound of the guitar). We talked about vintage pedals as compared to new, and how hard these things were to find. He asked if I would mind if he personally picked out a pedal for me at a local vintage guitar shop there in Austin where he had seen a couple of these pedals a short time before.

I told him he didn't have to but yet he insisted. You know the scenario, it was like oh come on Eric, you don't have to do that, and all the while you're thinking . . . this is incredible! Here's the "King of Tone" searching for the ultimate Tube Screamer pedal just for me! He went on to tell me that he was about to leave to play one show with Jeff Beck and afterward continue on with an entire tour with guitarist Joe Satriani the next week. In fact, he said that was the reason he didn't come out to hear me because the band had been rehearsing every night. He also told me there was nothing he needed at the music store but he'd love to go there and pick out a pedal for me. I said to my daughter Haley, "You know . . . I lose an ear and God gives me the very best ears in the world to go out and pick out an overdrive pedal for me! Isn't that just like the Lord to do something like that?" Eric told me he'd call me later that afternoon and let me know what he'd found.

"You know . . . I lose an ear and God gives me the very best ears in the world to go out and pick me out an overdrive pedal!"

I thought about it the entire afternoon. The only thing was, Eric didn't call me back that day. We have a tennis court in our backyard and this is where I would exercise and walk every day during my recovery period. I still do this when I'm home. I've never played tennis on it, but I could walk around and around for a mile or two and still be in my backyard and could always get back to the house during my recovery. I remember walking around on the tennis court and praying for Eric. I asked the Lord to bless him and said, "Lord, please bless Eric and do something special for him! He's going out of his way to bless me, but I feel he really needs a blessing himself. Just please do something special for Eric and show him that You love him!" A lot of prayers and divinely inspired ideas have become realities from my time talking with the Lord on that tennis court. I still do that every time I come home.

Doyle's "Boomerang" orange DDSM guitar. Notice the beautiful figured "birthday" quilted maple. See the rest of the story on page 95.

The next afternoon he called and apologized for not calling me back the day before. He kept emphasizing how he went over to the guitar shop just for me and had no other reason to go there, except to find that pedal for me. He said he had everything he needed for his upcoming tour and that he probably wouldn't have gone back there for several months. I thanked him once again. He told me he bought a pedal for me and wanted to give it to me as a gift. I was so humbled by this.

He went on to say, "Doyle, you don't understand. I was in the music store and went into this room with a guitar and amp and as I was trying out the pedals, I looked in the corner and saw three vintage guitars that looked very familiar to me. These looked like the guitars that had been stolen from me back in the mid-'80s. I went home to get the police report and all the serial numbers matched. I even had a *Guitar Player* magazine from that period with a section that read, 'If you see any of these guitars with these serial numbers, they were stolen from Eric Johnson.' This is the reason I didn't call you back yesterday afternoon. The store owner explained that the guitars were in quarantine and wouldn't have lasted twenty-four hours. In fact he already had an overseas buyer for at least one of them."

I asked him what kind of guitars they were and he said, "A '50s black custom color Fender Stratocaster, a '60s sunburst Stratocaster, and a '60s Gibson ES 335." These guitars were worth tens of thousands of dollars even if they

NO MATTER HOW MUCH I TRY TO LOOK LIKE A ROCK STAR . . . MY PHOTOS, LIKE MY GUITAR PLAYING, ALWAYS TURN OUT COUNTRY.

weren't connected to Eric, but since they had belonged to him I'm sure they were worth much more. Eric is known for playing and collecting vintage instruments. He told me that these were some of the best and most cherished guitars that he'd ever owned — and I'm thinking what better way could the Lord have blessed Eric Johnson and to show His love for him in such a personal way!

He said, "You had something to do with this, didn't you!" I told him I felt that this was bigger than either one of us and then he said, "This was Divine Providence, wasn't it?" I couldn't deny his claim and said there was no way to calculate that type of thing happening and he agreed. He said that the guitars had been brought in by a woman whose husband had passed away, and they had been stashed away under the bed or someplace and she brought them into the store to sell. I told him I believed it was indeed a "God thing" and how I believed God was going to give him favor with this lady and get his guitars back.

A few days later, Eric called me back and explained how the woman wouldn't take anything even though he offered her money. The only thing she would take was a copy of the *Guitar Player* magazine from the '80s that had the article about the guitar information. Later I saw these three guitars at Eric's studio in Austin when I recorded "All Be Done Dink" and "Red Clay" for my *Bridging the Gap* CD. Eric recorded "Red Clay" with me. I'll always cherish the favor and friendship of this incredibly talented musician.

I realize God can use anything and anyone, but sometimes He comes up with things that we simply cannot fit together and calculate in our minds and He'll use the most interesting means to carry it out, like vintage guitars — or even a lost coin or sheep. Joseph put his silver chalice in his brother's grain bag so they would bring them all back to him and he would reveal who he was and they would ultimately eat at the king's table! The fact is, He wants to draw us closer to Him. If we could look beyond the gift once again and focus on the Giver, we can fully understand it all.

In the most trying and difficult time of my life, I saw the Lights of Friendship, Compassion, and Favor. I believe this promoted healing for me. I also saw the lights of blessing from the "Father of Lights" to one of the most talented people I've ever met, Mr. Eric Johnson. And I believe Eric had an epiphany of God's love light shining on him that day.

Favorite Scriptures for this Chapter

Luke 6:38

"Give, and it will be given to you:
good measure, pressed down,
shaken together, and running over
will be put into your bosom. For with the
same measure that you use,
it will be measured back to you."

Matthew 10:42

"And whoever gives one of these little ones
only a cup of cold water in the name of a disciple,
assuredly, I say to you, he shall by
no means lose his reward."

*1994–My first Taylor
20th Anniversary
Rosewood*

CHAPTER 17

H

Hero Sandwiches

"Hero Sandwich" was the title of a song I wrote some years back and recorded it for my *Gitarre 2000* and *HEAT* albums. It was a song I wrote by borrowing the styles of Chet Atkins and Lenny Breau. I've met many of my heroes—guitar heroes, that is. Some people say you should never meet your heroes because you'll be disappointed. That's true with many people I've spoken to, but not with me. I've already mentioned Roy Clark, Eric Johnson, and James Burton. Here are a few more stories about some of my guitar heroes.

Merle Travis

I was raised in the home of a real guitar man, my dad "Bubba" Dykes. He loved Merle Travis, Les Paul, and Chet Atkins. Those were the "big three" in our world. When I auditioned for Grandpa Jones (if you want to call it auditioning), he asked if I picked like Merle Travis. I told him I always tried to. That's how I got the job.

GRANDPA JONES AND HIS OLD PAL AND GUITAR PLAYER, MERLE TRAVIS, BACKSTAGE AT THE GRAND OLE OPRY. THEY TREATED ME WITH WARMTH AND RESPECT. I REALLY STRIVE TO USE THEM AS ROLE MODELS.

One morning without warning, Grandpa Jones called me over to his home. When I answered the phone, he said, "Git over here, and bring that big guitar!" I had no idea what I was in for that day. I'd only dreamed about meeting someone like Merle Travis. To me he was bigger than life. As I was driving down Grandpa's long driveway to his home, I noticed a big white Cadillac with an Oklahoma license plate that said, "16-TONS." Suddenly my stomach hit the floorboard of the car as I knew I was about to meet Merle Travis, and I so did!

Merle took out his old Gibson Special Super 400 that had his famous name inlaid with mother-of-pearl in the fingerboard and handed it to me. Just to hold this legendary guitar was literally like holding a piece of country music history. Merle Travis wrote many songs such as "Sixteen Tons" and "Dark as a Dungeon," and was in lots of movies such as *From Here to Eternity* with Burt Lancaster, Deborah Kerr, and Frank Sinatra. He later became a member of the Country Music Hall of Fame. He influenced folks such as Chet Atkins and Scotty Moore (Elvis Presley's guitarist) and the list goes on. He asked me to play something and of course I played a Merle Travis song! (DUH!) Although he seemed flattered, I could tell he wanted to say something like, "Uh . . . do you know anything besides Merle Travis stuff?" He played my blond 1965 Gibson

L-5CESN, which was also a beautiful guitar. I bought it because it was so much like Merle Travis's guitar.

Merle spent the entire day with me showing me things and just jamming along. He had a unique way of playing finger-style guitar. He played with his thumb using a thumb-pick and his index finger. He told me he always thought of it like playing honky-tonk piano.

Grandpa Jones took out his treasured Nikon camera and took photos. None of the photos turned out. (Grandpa wasn't as good of a photographer as he was an entertainer.) However, he did record our "jam session" on an old reel-to-reel tape recorder and gave me the tape. I still have it and treasure it to this day.

That day I saw the lights of blessing and a reward from God that few young musicians would ever have. To some it was like meeting Elvis or the Beatles. To me, Merle Travis was bigger than life. Merle won my heart more than ever by his warmth and willingness to share his God-given gifts with me. He wasn't handing me a mantle or anything when he handed me his old guitar. He was simply giving me himself . . . Merle Travis.

Doyle's 1988 Del Vecchio

Chet Atkins

It had been years since I left Grandpa Jones and was pastoring the little church in Jacksonville. I had taken a mission trip to Brazil and brought back a Del Vecchio guitar for my old friend Steve Wariner, who is also now a member of the Grand Ole Opry and one of the finest players around today! These Del Vecchio guitars are rare, since they are made in Brazil. Only a handful of players were fortunate enough to own one since nowadays especially they are very difficult to get. Chet made the Del Vecchio famous on many of his recordings from the '60s until he passed away in 2001. I asked Steve if he thought Chet would like another one, and he in no uncertain terms explained how much he'd love it. The next time I went to Brazil, I went to two or three different stores and found the very best Del Vecchio guitar I could find. When I came back I sent it to Chet's office in Nashville.

Doyle's
1991 Gibson
Chet Atkins CE
signed by
Chet Atkins
(a gift from Chet)

I didn't hear from him for a while. In the meantime I'd left the church to start playing my guitar again and was going through a time when I was feeling pretty low about things. Sometimes Satan comes along to steal your confidence and self-esteem. Yet Jesus came to give us life and that more abundantly, and just when I needed to be reminded of that, Chet called me over to his office.

I'll never forget him walking down the steps holding one of his famous signature guitars he designed for the Gibson Guitar Company. He was talking as he walked down the steps and said, "Well, I've wondered what happened to you. I followed your career for a while and then I heard you went into church work. I admire you for that."

Here was arguably the most listened-to and copied guitarist of all time. People such as Jerry Reed, George Harrison, and Mark Knopfler (Dire Straits) have all credited Chet as one of their greatest influences. Aside from being a great guitarist and having recorded numerous solo guitar albums, Chet was perhaps even better known as a producer in Nashville. His awards are too numerous to mention, and here he was spending the afternoon with a young, guitar-picking preacher.

It was a couple of years later that I had the opportunity to see Chet several times in concert—which was something I always dreamed of. In 1997 I was asked to be on a show on the Grand Ole Opry. "Guitar Man Night" was telecast live on TNN. I stood on that famous stage between Chet Atkins and Duane Eddy and other heroes of mine—the Opry guitar trio, which was Jimmy Capps, Leon Rhodes, and Spider Wilson. How would you like to be sandwiched between Chet and Duane on the same show? Talk about a "Hero Sandwich"! And as I've mentioned before, I had the opportunity to play with Chet onstage again at Cafe Milano.

I had also written a script for a music video involving a song of mine called "Twin Six Shooters" that I recorded on Step One Records. Ray Pennington, the president and executive producer, approved the budget and my script as long as one of the characters would agree to be on it. The sheriff character was to be Chet. I called Chet personally to ask if he'd like to be on the video and he told me he'd love to but his health wasn't too good. He'd been pretty weak and felt he shouldn't take on any new projects. He told me he was in the middle of recording an album with a guitar player from Australia named Tommy Emmanuel. He explained how much of the work on the album was Tommy and how he'd been almost too weak to finish it. We found out later Chet had a tumor at that time and no doubt didn't realize it.

As I mentioned, I'll never forget this thin Southern gentleman from Tennessee whom I'd admired so many years walking down those steps in his office that day with his guitar in his hands. What I didn't tell you is the next thing he did was hand it over to me as a gift.

That day, I saw the lights of generosity and humility. These weren't attributes of my own but ones I saw in my childhood hero and my biggest hero to this day — Chet Atkins.

I'll also never forget the day I heard the news of Chet's passing. I was in Florida at my niece's wedding. My son Caleb ran out and told me as I had parked the car in the lot and was walking into the reception at the Sawgrass Clubhouse. I took him by the hand and we went into a flower garden and wept.

During the eight-hour drive home, I asked the Lord to allow me to do something to honor my hero. There were so many others, including Steve Wariner, Eddy Arnold, and Garrison Keillor, who were involved in the funeral service. The next morning after we arrived home, I got the call from Pete Fisher, general manager of the Grand Ole Opry. He explained how they were having a Tuesday night Opry show and were going to honor Chet. He asked if I'd play. That was the very day of his funeral.

Little Jimmy Dickens introduced me. I played a song for my friend Johnny Russell, who was a great singer and songwriter who had also passed away that day. When I played a medley of Chet Atkins songs, there was a huge photo of Chet behind me. It was shown later on national television as well as written up on syndicated news all around the country. God allowed me to honor this man who was my mentor and friend. My own father was also very proud that I was there since he was the man who turned me on to my childhood hero, teenage young adult hero, and now even as a grandpa, my biggest guitar hero — Chet Atkins.

Mr. James Burton

As I mentioned earlier in this book, I met James Burton when I was with the Stamps Quartet. He had such an unusual persona because on the one hand he had a friendly disposition, yet on the other, there was an element of superstar status since he'd recorded with everybody from Ricky Nelson, Merle Haggard, and Elvis to Johnny Mathis and Barbra Streisand. He took such control when he played his solos, especially when the spotlight would hit him playing his pink-paisley guitar. Elvis seemed to love showing him off to the crowd.

A few years ago I was playing at the Eric Clapton "Crossroads" festival in Dallas, Texas. They teamed me up with some pretty extraordinary folks such as James, Marty Stuart, Joe Osborne, and Jed Hughes. It was the day after President Reagan died and I started the show out with "The Patriotic Medley." The guys just stayed in the background and I finally motioned for them all to come out and join me on the last few choruses. Suddenly it turned into a Rockabilly Americana Salute to our president and our country and the crowd went wild! From there on out it was a "Round Robin" of chicken pickin' mania and just sheer entertainment. What an incredible show and incredible crowd. I truly do love Texas!

Doyle's 2006 Fender Telecaster James Burton Model (a gift from James Burton)

That day James asked if I would come and play at the first James Burton Foundation Guitar Festival. Since then, I've been the only guitarist to have been invited to the festival multiple times. James gave me a great compliment by saying when I play the guitar, God shows up and he said he'd rather have God's presence there than any superstar guitar hero. He was really giving all the glory to the Lord! What a privilege to have shared the stage with James Burton, Steve Wariner, Brad Paisley, Eric Johnson, Al Dimeola, Steve Lukather, Emmylou Harris, Kenny Wayne Sheppard, Steven Segal, Dickey Betts, Sonny Landreth,

 Mark Farner, Johnny Rivers, Phil Keaggy, and a host of others. The official emcee has been John Goodman for several years in a row. When Haley and I did "Amazing Grace," John Goodman wept!

I don't think I've ever met anyone as cool and debonair as Duane, yet he's one of the nicest men on the planet.

The James Burton Festival has given away literally thousands of guitars to those less fortunate. He and his wife, Louise, gave me thirty guitars to give to a charity or a special cause of my own choosing. I chose to give them to the elementary school where my brother, Aubrey, was the music teacher. I'll never forget the day my daughter Haley and I went to the school to give a concert and present the guitars to them. It was Halloween Day 2008. Aubrey also played the keyboard. When they opened the curtains to unveil the guitars, I experienced the loudest screams I'd heard since that time I saw Elvis in Fort Worth. There was so much excitement in the auditorium that day. My mother and father were there as well as my son-in-law Tom Dixon and my grandson Andrew. It was the last time Dad ever saw us play, and he seemed so proud. That was a blessing to me I'll never forget since Dad always loved to give to folks less privileged, and he instilled that in Aubrey and me.

He passed away three weeks later. What a nice way for us to have honored the Lord, my dad "Bubba" Dykes, and the gift of music and giving these guitars away by the help and devotion of one of my greatest guitar heroes — Mr. James Burton.

Duane Eddy

I first met Duane at the Grand Ole Opry. He was a more mature man than I remembered in the old photographs I saw of him but just as cool and handsome. He was Elvis on guitar! I don't think I've ever met anyone as cool and debonair as Duane, yet he's one of the nicest men on the planet. Duane and his wife, Deed, are two of the most-loved folks in the music business.

Duane walked out on the Opry stage with the beautiful blond Duane Eddy Model Guild guitar that I saw in the photographs when I was a teenager. Duane and I hit it off immediately and soon were in the studio recording together. He hired the players, two of whom I've used on several of my recordings, Dave Pomeroy on bass guitar and Steve Turner on drums. I spoke with Duane just this week to make plans on finishing our recording project. He's also on the song I wrote for this book, "The Lights of Marfa," which is on the e-book version with a video of us playing in the studio.

Doyle's 1958 Gretsch Chet Atkins 6120 "Transition"

Duane also recorded several times with me on my own CDs as well as a BMG project called *Sounds of Wood and Steel 3*, which also included other artists such as Phil Keaggy, Suzy Boggus, Jim Messina, and Dave Matthews. He also agreed to play "Duane Thang," a song I wrote for him on my latest DVD. The beautiful blond signature guitar he used on the taping

DUANE EDDY AND ME. YOU CAN'T OUT-COOL DUANE EDDY!

was destroyed in the 2010 Nashville flood along with several other treasured guitars. His original 6120 Gretsch that he used on so many of his hits was spared.

One of my favorite shows ever was a special tribute to Duane by Chet Atkins that also included other players such as Peter Frampton, John Fogerty, and Vince Gill. It was the first time I played at the Ryman Auditorium in Nashville, which was the home of the Grand Ole Opry for many years and still is today during the winter season. It was the last time Chet was on the Opry stage. We also played together to honor Chet at the Chet Atkins Appreciation

Society Convention. It was Chet's last time to attend the convention, and that night Chet played in public, also for the last time. These things run deep in our hearts when people are so loved and highly revered. Duane and I share these memories together, which to me is very special.

Once, Duane and I took Chet out to lunch. I quickly noticed that Duane was like a schoolboy around Chet. He dearly loved him, and I could see then that we shared the same guitar hero. Only thing is, Duane was a huge guitar hero as well. Duane is a member of the Rock and Roll Hall of Fame and a Grammy winner. His recordings have topped the charts and sold millions. He has appeared in several movies as well as having a string of top ten hits and many top recordings. His guitar playing has influenced people such as John Entwistle of the Who and the Beatles' George Harrison, and many others. He has been produced by Paul McCartney, Jeff Lynne, and other famous folks. He's rubbed shoulders with guys such as John Wayne, Elvis, Richard Boone, and Frank Sinatra.

Yet, with all this success one could easily see our lunch with Chet was a very special time for him. We talked about little things mostly. Duane brought up the time that he himself was on a television show "sandwiched" between two of his heroes, Chet and Les Paul. On live television the two "heroes" started arguing about their signature guitars because Duane's first guitar was a Les Paul gold top. Les said something like, "See, Chet, he went out and bought a Gibson Les Paul!" Chet responded with, "Yeah, but look what he traded it in for!" (This happened to be a Gretsch Chet Atkins model 6120 that he recorded the majority of his hits on.) That was also an afternoon I'll never forget!

I mentioned in an earlier chapter how I had a major operation a few years ago. I remember waking up and there was my wife, Rita, my brother, Aubrey . . . and Duane and Deed Eddy. That day I saw the lights of friendship—not fame and fortune. That day I saw a hero who was bigger than life and in some ways, bigger than any other guitar hero. I saw my friend and brother Duane Eddy.

Les Paul

I grew up with Les Paul and Mary Ford records being played weekly in our home. As I mentioned earlier in the book, he played his 1952 gold top and he'd intro the song much like a Les Paul and Mary Ford recording. I never thought I'd get to meet Les, but boy, did I! It was 1999 and I was in New York City. I had met up with my good friend and fellow musician and writer Jon Chappell at his home in Rye just north of the city. When we got off the train at Grand Central Station, he took me to Sam Ash Music where I purchased my first Les Paul guitar. We took a taxi to the Iridium Club where Les was playing. I was hoping to get to meet him to have him sign my new guitar so I looked around to see if my friend Tom Doyle (Les Paul's engineer and tech) was around.

Doyle's 1992 Gibson Les Paul 40th Anniversary (signed by Les Paul)

Not only was he around but he personally took me to Les's dressing room to meet him. I mentioned to Les how he was such a huge part of my musical heritage and such, but then I mentioned knowing Chet and he lit up like a Christmas tree! He asked if I'd get up and play with him on the second show, which I did. A year later I was there again; and then again a couple of years later. Each time, Les asked me to play. I remember playing things off the "Chester and Lester" albums. He played with me on "Lover Come Back to Me" and "Avalon."

When Les passed away I was called by my good friends Steve King and Johnnie Putman of the *Steve & Johnnie Show* on WGN radio in Chicago to tell personal stories of Les Paul on their show. I actually first met them backstage at the Grand Ole Opry. Les really loved Steve and Johnnie too and would sometimes call and talk with them after his Monday night gig until four or five in the morning. In fact, the first time I went to hear Les, there was a young couple sitting next to me. When they heard my name, the lady introduced herself as Steve and Johnnie's producer and immediately invited me on the show. That relationship with them has been a keynote relationship for me not only in my career but also in my personal circle of friends.

I saw the lights of opportunity to shine and honor the very One who gave us the gift of music.

When Les first called me up onstage to play with him, I saw this very cool elderly man with a smile like a Texan and a wit like a New York comedian. I also saw the lights of compassion and grace and imagined how wonderful God was to allow me to see such a legend. I saw the lights of opportunity to shine and honor the very One who gave us the gift of music through this living legend, Rock and Roll Hall of Famer, inventor, chart-topping Grammy winning artist, and television star. I saw the door of opportunity to shine. The thing was . . . no one could outshine Les and when you were around him, you didn't want to.

The next time I went to see Les was after 9/11. This time, instead of just honoring my guitar hero, I honored the New York police and firefighters and those who died on 9/11 and . . . well, when I played "How Great Thou Art" even Les was at a loss for words. The last time I was there I saw the lights of God's anointing and presence. There's no guitar hero who can come close to how that makes you feel. Somehow, I know Les would've agreed. I went back once more and again had the opportunity to play with one of my dad's and my biggest heroes . . . Les Paul.

People have said to me that they feel I've been handed down the mantle by carrying on some of the guitar styles of their heroes. I'm sure Tommy Emmanuel, Steve Wariner, Richard Smith, and others have heard the same thing. They feel there's been some sort of "transference" and in a way, I get that too. In the Bible, in 2 Kings 2, Elijah didn't hand his mantle to Elisha. He had been mentoring Elisha for ten years, but when God took Elijah up to heaven by a whirlwind, his mantle fell from him! Elisha picked the mantle up himself and God used it mightily. Personally, I don't feel I could carry these guys' guitar cases, so to speak, but I've picked up some things I feel were divinely given and with God's anointing, I believe I can be used of God and I expect that.

I believe the influence that Chet, Merle, Duane, and Les had on me has touched people in churches, concerts, festivals, guitar events, and even the Grand Ole Opry. I have other guitar heroes, too, like Duane Friend, Jerry Reed, Lenny Breau, Hank Garland, and Tommy Emmanuel. As I said before, meeting your heroes can sometimes be very disappointing. In my case, the lights came on for me and I think for them too. I sure was blessed by it all!

The guitar-slingin' heroes I've mentioned here are like the Lights of Marfa. They appear in the distance, then they get brighter and sometimes closer, and then they begin to dance. It's amazing to me that I've had the unique opportunity to join in on the fun!

FAVORITE SCRIPTURES FOR THIS CHAPTER

Proverbs 18:16

"A man's gift makes room for him,
and brings him before great men."

———✦———

First Chronicles 16:33

"Then shall the trees of the wood sing out
at the presence of the LORD, because he
cometh to judge the earth." (KJV)

———✦———

First Samuel 16:17–23

"So Saul said to his servants, 'Provide me now a man
who can play well, and bring *him* to me.' Then one of the servants
answered and said, 'Look, I have seen a son of Jesse the
Bethlehemite, who is skillful in playing, a mighty man of valor,
a man of war, prudent in speech, and a handsome person;
and the LORD is with him.' Therefore Saul sent messengers to Jesse,
and said, 'Send me your son David, who is with the sheep.'
And Jesse took a donkey loaded with bread, a skin of wine,
and a young goat, and sent them by his son David to Saul.
So David came to Saul and stood before him. And he loved him greatly,
and he became his armorbearer. Then Saul sent to Jesse, saying,
'Please let David stand before me, for he has found favor in my sight.'
And so it was, whenever the spirit from God was upon Saul,
that David would take a harp and play it with his hand.
Then Saul would become refreshed and well,
and the distressing spirit would depart from him."

1994–My first Taylor
20th Anniversary Rosewood

CHAPTER 18

Riding Off into the Sunset

I enjoy collecting old Western movies starring John Wayne, Gene Autry, and Roy Rogers; and television series such as Steve McQueen's *Wanted: Dead or Alive*, as well as *The Lone Ranger, Bonanza,* and *The Rifleman.* I especially love the old cliché ending of how the cowboy hero rides off into the sunset. Although "THE END" is splashed across the screen, we all know this isn't really the ending but only the beginning of a new adventure in this continuing saga.

Perhaps that is precisely what this book will mean for you! In fact, it is my desire and prayer that this will open a new chapter to the most exciting days of your life—that you will be "illuminated."

So, all this started way back when I was that eleven-year-old boy saying to God, "Lord, if You'll give me a job to do, I'll always tell people about You!" That's right, for me it wasn't the guitar that came first . . . and it still isn't. I'm trying to tell you about Him.

The first time I played as a solo artist was when I played special music in an old cleaned-out chicken barn. (Actually it wasn't all that cleaned out . . .) I picked guitar and my pastor Wayne Proctor was going to preach. As it turned out, he asked me to give my testimony that night. I'll have to say it was the smelliest church I'd ever played in!

I suppose I did a lot of "chicken pickin'" that night. Three roosters were saved and an old hen laid an egg! (Sorry for that!) I thought to myself, *What in the world am I doing here?* But since then I've heard from two fellows, one now pastoring in Illinois and another in Alabama, who were there, in the chicken barn, that night. The guy from Illinois told me he got saved at that concert, and the Alabama preacher is a fine guitarist. So chicken barn or not, God was definitely up to something that night.

WE ALL KNOW THAT THIS ISN'T REALLY THE END BUT ONLY THE BEGINNING OF A NEW ADVENTURE IN THIS CONTINUING SAGA.

As you've already seen, I've met most of my heroes and performed onstage or played casually with them. I've played my guitar in some of the smallest (and now you know . . . smelliest) as well as the largest venues in the United States and many stages in some of the most beautiful places in the world. I've seen some strange and wonderful sights! Stonehenge in England; the Highlands and Borders of Scotland; the Lake District of England; the magnificent churches and castles of Europe; the Alps of Switzerland and Italy; the seaside cities of beautiful Scandinavia; the lush green hills of Ireland; the skyline at Kowloon Bay in Hong Kong; the Christ the Redeemer statue in Rio de Janeiro; Mt. Fuji in Japan; the fishing villages in Melbourne; the Sydney Harbor Bridge and Opera House; the bright lights of Tokyo and towering skyscrapers of Shanghai; beautiful New Zealand; the Caribbean islands; the vast savannas of South Africa; the Manila American Cemetery and Memorial in the Philippines; Genbaku Dome (or the A-Bomb Dome) in Hiroshima; the famous Brandenburg Gate in Berlin; and unbelievable sights in all fifty states of our own beautiful nation—including the Lights of Marfa.

Once I visited an ancient Buddhist temple in Shanghai. As I strolled out into the beautiful watered gardens that were connected to the temple, I looked and to my complete surprise, I saw a miracle right before my eyes. It was a Starbucks coffee shop! (When you're a coffee snob like me, you know that had to be a God thing!) I've laid my head on a pillow at night in every continent in the world except the one way, way down south and I don't think there are many penguins who dig guitar playing! I've never felt that I didn't have the Lord with me. His promise to us is that He will never leave us or forsake us. I've never felt alone.

Life has never been boring to me. I really feel I'm living the "abundant life." Sure, sometimes life can seem unfair and things come along that can be very un-heavenly. I heard Pastor Rick Warren speaking on the Lord's Prayer and he said, "Jesus instructed us to pray, Thy kingdom come, Thy will be done . . . on Earth as it is in Heaven . . . because otherwise, it simply isn't that way, folks!

Why do you think He told us to pray that way if we had Heaven on Earth every day?" After his message I came onstage and played "The Lord's Prayer." What a beautiful thing that was for me to experience.

As I explained earlier in the chapter "A Compassionate Friend," I had an operation a few years ago that resulted in what some call "brain surgery." Well, I deal with things even today as a result of that, but I still love and trust God and wouldn't trade my Christian experience for anything in the world. I lost hearing in my right side because of this tumor that was in my head. They had to compress my brain (Rita said, "But not much!") in order to get at it with the procedure I chose, which was the only way I had even a slight chance of keeping my hearing in my right ear.

Sometimes I don't get it, but I lost the one thing I suffered so much trying to keep! The residual headaches from the surgery were almost unbearable and came at random times while I was on the road. I felt like, "God, either heal me or take me home!" (I even said that a couple of times, but I think He thought I meant "home in Tennessee" because I'm still here, although the headache problem is better.) I actually held off writing this book a couple of years, waiting for the last chapter, which I hoped would be that I got my hearing back. I'm still believing for my hearing miracle, and I say that with great anticipation and as a statement of faith. However, I still thank God that His "Goodness and Mercy" follows ME all the days of MY life. He gives us Joy . . . that Joy that is our strength. He gives us Peace . . . His Peace that keeps our hearts and minds in Christ Jesus! The only Righteousness we have is HIS Righteousness!

I'm thankful I can still hear well enough to play my guitar. I have a friend who had a similar operation, except he had it twice. He lost his hearing completely. He still loves Jesus and is writing his own book about it. He's also one of Bob Taylor's closest friends, and Bob tells me he was the most amazing drummer that he's ever had the privilege of working with. His name is Tim Mauricio and he emails me regularly to ask how he can pray for me! Friends, to me Tim's light shines brighter than any I've seen out on a desert floor! You could call it "The Lights of Mauricio"!

Jesus said in John 16:33 (AMP), "I have told you these things, so that in Me you may have [perfect] peace and confidence. In the world you have tribulation and trials and distress and frustrations; but be of good cheer [take courage: be confident, certain, undaunted]! For I have overcome the world. [I have deprived it of power to harm you and have conquered it for you.]"

My good friend retired FBI agent John Hall, a guitar player and instructor at Quantico at the FBI Academy, was presented an award by the Texas Rangers for some work he did for them. The inscription reads: "No man in the wrong can stand up against a fellow that's in the right when he keeps on a-comin'." God has always been there for me and He just keeps on a-comin'! God has never failed me and He won't fail you either!

Doyle's 2007 Custom R. Taylor "The Tree"

We may never have all the answers to things in this life. The good thing is, I believe in heaven as much as I do earth and I believe someday I'll see my dad and a lot of my old heroes once again! I believe I'll see First Sergeant Aaron D. Jagger once again, and we'll play guitars together. It is that blessed hope—and that's what heaven is all about.

Sometimes the Lord gives us a glimpse of that reality. Life in some ways provides "the viewing area" and Jesus paid the price in full for you to be able to see the light of God's love and grace. Just like in Marfa, you just have to make the decision to see for yourself. That's what this book is about.

I've had so many great experiences in my life but nothing comes close to that day in 1965 when the light of the glorious gospel shone deep inside my heart and my life was transformed. In other words . . . I was saved that day! The main way to get saved is to realize you need saving. We were born in sin so everyone needs a Savior! That explains the verse "For God so loved the world that He gave His only begotten Son, that whoever believes in Him should not perish but have everlasting life. For God did not send His Son into the world to condemn the world, but that the world through Him might be saved" (John 3:16–17).

My mother and father used to read these verses to me when I was a little boy. I didn't understand it all then, but still those words were comforting to me. When I was in Sunday school I learned this: "That if you confess with your mouth the Lord Jesus and believe in your heart that God has raised Him from the dead, you will be saved. For with the heart one believes unto righteousness, and with the mouth confession is made unto salvation" (Romans 10:9–10). Maybe these are verses you also have heard and learned since you were a child, but perhaps you haven't read them for a while. Maybe somewhere you drifted away from it but just now, reading this has also caused the lights to come on once again. The reason for this is these words are truth and they are real and they will set you free.

The things I've told you in this book are all true and real and I believe they were given to me to give affirmation to what I already know is true and real. I believe this is true and real: "Jesus loves me this I know, for the Bible tells me so!" If you believe this too, then simply ask God to forgive your sins and accept you right where you are and then just confess Him as Lord of your life. That means giving Him "Supreme Authority" over you! If you're concerned about your lifestyle or bad habits and hang-ups, don't worry about all that! When you give yourself to Him, you're giving Him all that too! No one is good enough to go to heaven on their own; that's why we need a Savior, and that Savior is Jesus Christ! Trust Him to help you with the rest. Jesus gave Himself — all that He is — for you, so you should give yourself — all that you are — to Him. No matter what lifestyle you've had in the past, just receive Christ right where you are and how you are and you can have "the Style of Life" you were created for! Let God do His perfect work in you! Remember, "He's the potter and you're the clay!" Relax and trust Him that His plan and His will is the best thing for you. As far as your lifestyle or old habits . . . my friend Pastor Greg Laurie always put it like this: "Jesus always cleans his fish AFTER He catches them!"

Years ago I left my parents' home to drive the forty-five-minute trip across town to our new place in south Jacksonville. On the way, I penned these lyrics to a brand-new song. The song describes this humble little person, and I didn't know who this little guy was until the last line of the song. The words came so quickly I could hardly write them down fast enough.

The Man in the Lighthouse

Every day he cleans the lighthouse . . .
He polishes the lens,
He's learned all the instructions,
To make his beacon shine again,
Every day his light will shine,
Perhaps through troubled winds,
And if a storm is raging,
He'll guide another in.

For many generations,
His family's served it well,
He's never asked anything in return,
He's just glad if he can help,
Another soul that's gone astray,
Perhaps this is his day,
He'll shine his light through the harbor,
And get another saved.

He's the Man in the Lighthouse,
His job may not seem great,
But no one would ever know,
The difference that he's made,
To the souls out in the harbor,
Without him they would have died,
The Man in the Lighthouse . . .
Is You and I

I realize those lyrics "ain't grammatically correct" but I think you understand the meaning. The family I was writing about here that took care to maintain the lighthouse and its purpose is the family of God. Perhaps this book *The Lights of Marfa* is like a beacon in a lighthouse pointing you to God! If you've been searching, could it be this is the "searchlight" you've needed and longed for and you've been found? Jesus is still the answer! Whatever you've gone through or whatever you're going through now, God knows and understands and already has the answer calculated in the equation of your life.

If this is the case, then maybe for the first time in the history of the knowledge of the Marfa lights, there's a true reason for their existence. If only one person who reads this book will turn to the light of the glorious Gospel of Jesus Christ, then there's nothing random about the Marfa lights at all! Sometimes we need something else to hold on to. Jesus spoke in parables and often used little object lessons such as a flower or a little bird to get His message across. Sometimes we need confirmation—a sign—substance we can cling to. Remember in the story of the little white rose, how Heidi said, "But Daddy, I want one I can hold in my hand!" "Now faith is the substance of things hoped for, the evidence of things not seen" (Hebrews 11:1).

Maybe for the first time in the history of the knowledge of the Marfa lights, there's a true reason for their existence.

That little blessing has helped my family and me through a lot of troubled times. It has also given us an assurance in a personal way of God's love and care. He cares about you and the things that you need right now. God's forgiveness is bigger and better than anything you could ever imagine. Ask Him into your heart. If the "lights" don't come on immediately, they will, and the light of God's love and grace will never fade away! When you ask Him into your heart, your eternity with Him starts right now. Though we are not in heaven yet, God's grace will carry you until you get to heaven and then forevermore. As the old song says, "His Grace has brought me safe thus far . . . and Grace will lead me home."

It may be hard for you to comprehend, but that's what this book is all about. Some things you just know "in your knower" are true and real and go beyond human understanding. Every

"If you don't feel you're worth very much . . . then how come you cost God so much?"

harsh word you've spoken, every bad thing you've done, is forgotten. The Bible says God casts our sins as far as the east is from the west. God isn't "forgetful"; He's "forgiveful."

Now, you may not feel you're worth all this. My old friend and pastor Roy Nail once told me, "If you don't feel you're worth very much . . . then how come you cost God so much?" God gave His only begotten Son, and Jesus gave Himself freely to die for your sins. The King of kings and Lord of lords came down to our level from His throne—to raise us up to sit together with Him in the heavenly places (Ephesians 2:5–6). That's the Good News! That's the Gospel of Jesus Christ!

I believe anything that comes from God is eternal. God promises to give us wisdom, knowledge, understanding, peace, joy, love, creativity, His grace and forgiveness—and even music! Psalm 33:3 (KJV) says, "Sing unto him a new song; play skilfully with a loud noise." A good amplifier helps with that last part (HA!) but this verse proves that all the songs will not be written in this life. There will always be "new" songs!

(Just a comment here: A famous songwriter approached my old pal Grandpa Jones at a music event a number of years ago. He told

Grandpa he'd like to pitch a song to him. Grandpa said, "Wrote a new one, eh? What's it to the tune of?")

This book has a "theme song" — a new song I wrote called "The Lights of Marfa," setting to music my thoughts and feelings the day I saw the Marfa lights. The day we recorded this song in Nashville, I was amazed at the way the other musicians interacted with the song that I had had in my head for weeks, how they expressed their abilities and feelings through their music in the song. I don't like to tell good musicians how and what to play. That's why I always get other musicians that I feel are better than me, spurring me on to play my best! But at the same time, as we were all learning the song and making changes, I was reminded of how we're all still learning. There's more music in my guitar than I'll ever be able to play or create in this life. I'm convinced I'll still be playing my guitar in heaven.

Not everyone can play an instrument or sing like my daughter Haley did on that song, but everyone can experience the gift of God's grace and forgiveness — and it will create a new song in your heart. I promise you that! When it does, I believe you'll feel just like I did when I was eleven and raised my hands to God and said, "Give me a job and I'll always tell people about You!"

There's more music in my guitar than I'll ever be able to play or create in this life.

I'll never forget holding that little white rose in my hand, or the time Dr. Henry showed up next to me on that plane, or the Tennessee state trooper stopping me, or meeting Mr. Stringfield in his cowboy hat, or getting Eric Johnson's call about his guitars, or hearing the warning from the little blue-eyed preacher. None of these events happened randomly. I sincerely believe each was directed by the Holy Spirit. But I've also learned to look for these kinds of things.

These are the "dancing, shimmering, and colorful lights" that can't be explained or calculated but all point to one truth: God is there and He loves me.

That cold night in February 2010, as I rode off into the west Texas sunset, I went straight to the viewing area, expecting to see something—and I did. I saw the Lights of Marfa.

But if you want to experience the Light of Life, the Cross of Calvary is the viewing area and Jesus paid for it in full. Let's go out there now. Simply pray this prayer with me:

Heavenly Father,

Thank You for sending Jesus so that I could also have Your love and light in my life . . .

Holy Spirit,

Thank You for Your direction and for pointing me to Jesus . . .

Jesus,

Thank You for the cross — the viewing area of life. I want to experience Your light in me. Please forgive me for all my sins and accept me right where I am right now. I give You myself: my time, my talents, my dreams, all that I am — because You gave us Your all when You suffered and died for our sins.

Thank You for accepting me as I accept You as my Lord and Savior right now! In Jesus' name, amen.

If you prayed that prayer with me and believed this in your heart, then you are indeed saved. You don't have to be in a church or a cathedral for this to become a reality — remember the "chicken barn church" and how people's lives were changed and they left with a new life and a new beginning? That's what you have now too! It may be quiet where you are now, but there's a party going on in heaven right now!

Someday, we'll see the Lights of Heaven with colors beyond anything we've ever seen before. And then we'll see . . . the Father of Lights!

Now, let's ride together!

Favorite Scriptures for This Chapter

Ephesians 3:20–21
Now to Him Who, by (in consequence of) the
[action of His] power that is at work within us,
is able to [carry out His purpose and] do superabundantly,
far over and above all that we [dare] ask or
think [infinitely beyond our highest prayers, desires,
thoughts, hopes, or dreams] — To Him be glory in the church
and in Christ Jesus throughout all generations
forever and ever. Amen (so be it).

Matthew 5:16
"Let your light so shine before men,
that they may see your good works and
glorify your Father in heaven."

John 8:12
"Then Jesus spoke to them again,
saying, 'I am the light of the world.
He who follows Me shall not walk in darkness,
but have the light of life.'"

To watch Doyle play "Amazing Grace,"
pop in your DVD or go to
www.doyledykes.com/tlom.htm

To hear Doyle share what he hopes you'll take
away from the book, pop in your DVD or go to
www.doyledykes.com/tlom.htm

[APPENDIX]

Especially for Guitar Players:
Doyle Answers Your Questions

Q. Do you ever feel like the guitar is "not your friend"—that there are times you just don't feel like playing?

A. I always want to play, but there are ways to "keep it fresh." First, play what you want and you'll want to play. Merle Travis's son, Tom Bresh, once told me that his dad may have made up the term "playing" the guitar since it always seemed he was playing when he had a guitar in his hands. I realize some musicians may have formal lessons and assignments from instructors. In that case, it's even more important that you don't get so involved in your rigorous training exercises that you lose your first love to play the instrument. So, always take time to play what you feel and keep it fun and I believe you'll continue to grow and learn new things as well.

Q. How do you maintain your instruments?

A. If you keep your guitars in great playing condition, you'll enjoy playing them even more. I actually enjoy cleaning my guitar and changing strings regularly. I polish my guitar with spray-on instant wax-and-shine auto polish and also clean the fingerboard, although I don't condition the fretboard but once a year. Here's a more comprehensive list.

- Change strings regularly.

- Keep guitar clean and polished.

- Hydrate your guitar and keep a constant level of humidity.

- Store your guitar in its case.

- Keep the truss rod adjusted and a good action that feels right for you.

- Play in an environment that allows you to enjoy the sound of your guitar acoustically, such as a room in your home with hardwood or tile floors.

Q. How else can a guitar player "keep it fresh"?
A. Here are some ideas to try:

- Always try new things; keep your repertoire fresh with new songs. Try writing your own songs as well.

- Play to others besides yourself. Playing in your bedroom is fun but not challenging. Stretch yourself by playing to an audience, whether it's one or two people or two thousand people. This will help you get to the next level in your playing.

- Read magazines and watch videos of other players. Keep your knowledge of the guitar sharp and keep up with what other players are doing by watching YouTube and other videos.

- Find other players to collaborate with. I just recently recorded a song in a major studio with some of Nashville's finest players. In 2011, I am also playing a tour with Tommy Emmanuel and will be working with Dennis Agajanian, Phil Keaggy, and a host of players such as Ricky Skaggs, Roy Clark, and Eric Johnson on my new television series. I realize not everyone can have the opportunity to play with some of these guys—but I never thought I would either. So, keep stretching yourself by playing with other players who you're convinced are even better than you.

- Try new guitars. Whether you can buy a new one or just go into a music store and try one out, it will help you keep your interest and enthusiasm. Go to guitar shows such as trade shows or vintage guitar shows and festivals where luthiers are showing their wares. Keep up with your favorite manufacturers and try different wood tones, and you'll find that the acoustic guitar has as many variables in tone as playing an electric with a bunch of different effects pedals.

- Try alternate tunings. Go to different websites or check out some tab books or magazines with information from other players you admire and try some of their tunings for yourself. One fellow told me that he played more like Chet Atkins as he just played in standard tuning. Well, I'll have you know that Chet was experimenting around as well as arranging songs and recording them even in the 1950s using alternate tunings. This will also bring another dimension to your music.

- Go back and play some of your old arrangements and keep yourself familiar with them. Even though you may get tired of some of your old standards, others may not. I'm saying this to myself as well because if I'm not careful, I'll leave out some of the songs that people will come out and expect to hear me play.

- Stretch your fingers and tendons in your arms. I've written a couple of articles that I actually had an orthopedic surgeon cowrite concerning this subject. There are simple stretching exercises that can keep your arms and hands comfortable enough so that you can play to your heart's content.

- Record yourself with audio and video. This is not only a great way to critique yourself, but also you can help support your "habit" of buying more guitars by selling CDs and DVDs and such. I always keep a project such as this on the "back burner" because this way you're always thinking of it and looking for new things to keep your music fresh and interesting to others.

Originally published in Acoustic Magazine, *www.acousticmagazine.com.*

'HOW MANY GUITARS DO I NEED? ONE MORE.'
QUOTE FROM JOHN HALL: LAWYER, FIREARMS SPECIALIST,
AUTHOR, LECTURER, FBI AGENT (RETIRED), AND GUITAR MAN

Special Thanks

I thank God for this book. It was truly the orchestration and work of the Holy Spirit that created these stories. I'm so thankful that Jesus Christ is Lord of my life!

Special thanks to my wife, Rita, our children, Heidi, Holli, Haley, and Caleb, and their families. I've been away so much of their lives traveling and playing my guitar. I'm not proud of that, but I am proud of them. My family is my greatest blessing. They are my own personal Marfa lights. Where in the world could they have come from? They're not of this world!

To my parents, B.A. and Martha Dykes, and my brother, Aubrey Dykes. My father "Bubba" is with the Lord but he remains alive in my heart. (I would mention his real name but I believe even the Lord would address him as "Bubba.") My grandfather, W.B. Dykes, who asked me to play my first guitar solo in 1966.

I also want to thank my daughter Holli for all the great photos in this book and Haley for her amazing voice on "The Lights of Marfa" song and Duane Eddy, Dave Pomeroy, and all the Nashville pickers who played on it.

To my friend Steve Lyon, without whose vision, encouragement, and recommendation this book would have never been written. Also, to Elizabeth Newenhuyse, Holly Kisly, and the entire Moody Publishers staff in Chicago.

To my friend Bob Taylor. Thank you for telling me about Marfa, Texas, and for the many life-changing events that have come through our friendship. Also, to Kurt Listug and the entire Taylor Guitars family.

To Thilo Kramny and Dr. Michael Peters, whose adventurous spirits made me look toward Marfa, Texas, and wonder why they would travel thousands of miles to go there.

To Mike Robertson, Neal Ferry, and Roy Nail. Their partnership in ministry and music keeps me going literally around the world.

To my Texas friends—Del Way, Pastor Roy Cragg, Mark Pollock, and the folks in Marfa, Texas. I encourage everyone to go visit Marfa and see the lights! Better pack an extra lunch and fill your gas tank first!

To Darrell Owens, Kirk Sand, Nathan York, Doug Young, Jim Coker, David Lorency, Roger Daniels, Charlie Daniels (of Fresno), Rev. Steve Grandy, Wayne Charvel, Johnny Davis, John Mc Claren, and T.J. Baden. These were my California buddies who encouraged me to keep pickin' before anyone else found out I could.

—Doyle Dykes

I HAD TO FIND THE UGLIEST WALL IN TOWN TO TRY AND MAKE ME LOOK GOOD.

doyledykes.com

Doyle Dykes Productions
P.O. Box 5358 Cleveland, TN 37320